O God Our Help In Ages Past

O God Our Help in Ages Past

*A Theology of History for a Church
in a Troubled World*

JEFF BARNES

WIPF & STOCK · Eugene, Oregon

O GOD OUR HELP IN AGES PAST
A Theology of History for a Church in a Troubled World

Copyright © 2018 Jeff Barnes. All rights reserved. Except for brief quotations in critical publications or reviews, no part of this book may be reproduced in any manner without prior written permission from the publisher. Write: Permissions, Wipf and Stock Publishers, 199 W. 8th Ave., Suite 3, Eugene, OR 97401.

Wipf & Stock
An Imprint of Wipf and Stock Publishers
199 W. 8th Ave., Suite 3
Eugene, OR 97401

www.wipfandstock.com

PAPERBACK ISBN: 978-1-5326-4858-8
HARDCOVER ISBN: 978-1-5326-4859-5
EBOOK ISBN: 978-1-5326-4860-1

Manufactured in the U.S.A.   10/24/18

Scripture quotations are from the ESV® Bible (The Holy Bible, English Standard Version®), copyright © 2001 by Crossway, a publishing ministry of Good News Publishers. Used by permission. All rights reserved.

For my wife

"Remember this and stand firm,
recall it to mind, you transgressors,
remember the former things of old;
for I am God, and there is no other;
I am God, and there is none like me,
declaring the end from the beginning
and from ancient times things not yet done,
saying, 'My counsel shall stand,
and I will accomplish all my purpose,
calling a bird of prey from the east,
the man of my counsel from a far country,
I have spoken, and I will bring it to pass;
I have purposed, and I will do it.'"

—ISAIAH 46:8–11

Contents

Acknowledgements

FOR ANY AUTHOR, WRITING a book is a great endeavor that at some point swallows the author whole before it is completed. To write this book at this stage in my life, as I am completing my PhD and juggling that with teaching responsibilities and parenting (at one point in the process, six children), has required the aid and support of more people than space will permit me to thank. For those not listed here, know that I owe you a great debt of gratitude for whatever role you have played in keeping my sanity through this work. At the outset, I must thank my incredible students. This project began as part of my conversations with them about why the study of history is important for Christians. Many of the insights I offer here were first developed, and then refined, as part of these classroom discussions.

Academically, I could not be more fortunate to be surrounded by some of the best historians (who also happen to be some of the best human beings!) I have ever met. My undergraduate professors at Malone, all of whom I now teach alongside, first gave me my love for history, and centered that love in a kingdom mentality. Greg Miller modeled academic rigor for me, a lesson for which I am greatly indebted; he also provided me with my first opportunity to teach a history course to Christian students. Jay Case's witty and insightful comments on my writing as a lowly undergrad continue to guide me even after more than a decade has passed. A special debt of gratitude goes to Jacci Stuckey, who has modeled faith and professionalism for me in a way I only dream of doing some day. When deciding on my future vocation, I told myself that, when I grew up, I wanted to be like Dr. Stuckey, and her example continues to guide me. Affectionately, I have always maintained that it was Scott Waalkes who "ruined my life," causing me to fall in love with the Middle East and leave my math degree behind to pursue history (though he himself is a political scientist). This book, which cites his very insightful manuscript, would not exist without him. My very gifted advisor at Akron, Dr. Janet Klein, has been not only a source of academic inspiration but also a supportive friend, who has combined the right measures of toughness and compassion that have made me the scholar I am today. Countless others at Akron have mentored me first through my MA and now in my PhD, and though many of them are not believers, the insight they have given me into the historical process can be felt throughout this book.

Much of this manuscript was written, edited, and rewritten at the cabin owned by my mother and step-father. Their gracious invitation for me to use it without charge, whenever I needed, to work on this and other projects, unencumbered by children, has been invaluable. My mother has been one of the great lights of my life; she led me to the faith and turned my faith into action through her steadfast example, and her faith and wisdom are echoed in the following pages. My faith was further nurtured by my now-departed grandmother's prayers, which continue to be answered in my life through pursuits like this book. The support of the rest of my family, including my father's humor during our frequent conversations, which has kept me laughing during difficult days of writing, also helped keep this project alive.

The two years during which I wrote the draft of this manuscript were the most challenging of my life. Four foster children came into our home and left, sometimes painfully, and the trials and travails of that process are reflected in the theology of this book. I will never forget the legacies R, A, R, and O left in my life, and my love for all of them continues to grow, regardless of where they are now.

The support and encouragement of friends and our extended church family kept me going through these challenging times as well. In particular, I owe a great debt of gratitude to our "inner circle" of couples: Jonathan and Jen, Shane and Jillian, Stephen and Trisha, Jeremy and Liz, and Kyle and Kristen, as they have shared in every one of our afflictions, cared for our children in my frequent absences, and shared life with us in a way that only fellow believers can. Adam Romans, our very gifted and godly pastor, has shaped this book in ways he may never know. In particular, his reading of Elimelech's role in the Ruth narrative has found its way into the second chapter, though most of the book has been shaped by his careful teaching of the word. Tony Hanmer, who I first met in the mountains of the Republic of Georgia a decade ago, has been a constant encouragement and inspiration, and our reunion in Tbilisi while I was writing this book strengthened me to see it to the finish line. Finally, I would be remiss to not mention the scores of friends I have met in my travels in Palestine, many of whom possess a lived faith that has shaped my thinking about faith and history. Shadia, Shireen, and Salim in particular have taught me more in their lives about how God works in the historical process than any text I read in preparation for writing.

Finally, this process (as with much of my academic work) has both taken a toll on and been aided by my immediate family. Our oldest daughter Myana has been a constant source of strength and inspiration to me, keeping a smile on my face and holding me through all my tears. Ayla Lily has been gifted by God with a great love of his word and with an encouraging spirit, and her constant kind words kept me motivated when I wanted to stop writing. Judah has been, as he puts it, my best friend, a little guy who is truly becoming a man after God's own heart. Kenny, our oldest son, came into our lives during the dark times of the past year, and has brought me so much joy, hope, and love in a season of loss (though perhaps it may have been helpful if I would have spent the countless hours playing board games with him writing instead!).

Lastly, words cannot express the support, love, and encouragement I have derived from my wife, Carley, to whom this work is affectionately dedicated. From editing all of my work before submitting, to very difficult conversations debating the theological aspects of this book, to being an amazing example for our children, for all of the ways in which she touches every life that surrounds her, I cannot overstate how deeply this book reflects her. Her love has sustained me through the challenges of the past two years, and there is no one else with whom I would rather being doing life.

Soli deo gloria.

Introduction

"In Christian theology a view of history is closely allied to a concept of God. The language we use in speaking of God expresses in the barest metaphor what we feel about history. And the way we experience history—whether as open, hopeful, determined, fatalistic, or tragic—is an elaboration upon our concept of God; it is, in many ways, the most practical index to our true theological perspective."[1]

"Concisely, then, Christ is the meaning of history for the Christian."[2]

"Now these things happened to them as an example, but they were written down for our instruction, on whom the end of the age has come." (1 Cor 10:11)

TEACHING GENERAL EDUCATION WORLD history courses for a small Christian liberal arts school, I was greeted at the start of every semester by a classroom full of students who would rather be anywhere—literally *anywhere*—else. The few faces that greeted me that were not already bored were those that betrayed the excitement of finally being away from home. What was certain was that, with rare exception, none were excited to be here. To get to know one another, I asked students to explain why they were taking my class. The inevitable answer always shattered the optimist in me. Rather than a sweeping declaration of the value of history to their

1. Conyers, *God, Hope, and History*, 3.

2. Lewry, *Theology of History*, 59.

1

lives, most said something along the lines of "I had to take this class. It really doesn't have anything to do with my major."

These were good students, from strong educational backgrounds, who strongly desired to expand their knowledge and grow their faith. Most of them were excited to be at college and expressed delight in taking classes related to their field of study. A majority were strong Christians, people who passionately lived out and defended their faith. Yet with rare exception, few felt that studying the history of the entire human race over the past 500 years merited even a cursory amount of their time.

This is a pattern I have encountered more broadly in Christian circles. Inevitably, when I introduce myself to other Christians and explain to them that I am a historian, I am met with recalcitrance, or a swift "That was one of my least favorite subjects in school." This is usually accompanied by a furrowed brow that politely conveys the sentiment: "But when are you going to get a *real* job?" Even Christians who profess an interest in history often see it as a hobby, an incidental part of life that one can pick up to pass the time, along the same lines as gardening or fishing. Certainly it is not something that is integral to being a person of faith.

I have experienced the same apathy among my largely non-Christian students at the public universities at which I have taught. We live in a culture that is increasingly turning away from the humanities, a society in which universities and politicians push for the study of more "practical" subjects, such as the hard sciences. We have lost a sense of the real impact of the past on the present as we craft our identities in the here-and-now, through the banality of social media and what is currently trending, rather than drawing from the reservoir of the past to situate ourselves within the human story.

This is a tragedy for our society and, more specifically, a tragedy for the church. As Christians, we are adherents of a historical faith centered on a historical figure. What is more, this historical object of our worship—the incarnate word of God—is the person upon whom all of history turns. His arrival still bisects our dating system, and his influence on history extends throughout the ages.

He is the Lord of history, and the broad expanse of the human story is subsumed under his rule and will. When we begin to fully understand the significance of history to our faith and the centrality of our faith for comprehending history, then we discover that there is much to be gained for us as persons of faith from a study of the past. As we lurch forward into the information age and privilege the future over the past, we need to be reminded of history's significance for us. We need history to ground us, to provide us a vehicle through which we can begin to gain a sense of our own context as it has unfolded as part of the larger human story. We need to learn to make history a part of our daily lives, to begin to see ourselves as historical creatures, practitioners of a historical faith, and members of a society with a rich and complex history that spans well past our own blip on the radar of time. We need to begin to see history as a meaningful part of our lives, a necessary accompaniment to our faith formation, and as so much more than a mere intellectual curiosity.

THE RELATIONSHIP BETWEEN FAITH AND HISTORY

The central argument of this book is that a knowledge of the past, of history, is a central means through which Christians can come to know God better. As a worshipping community, we are a historical people, born out of the greatest events in human history—the incarnation and resurrection—and need to reclaim our historical awareness. It is my heart to see Christians treat history not as a mere intellectual object, a curiosity to be picked up by an inquisitive few. No, history is much more powerful than that. History must become a part of the outworking of our faith, an essential part of every Christian's walk.

As I often emphasize to my students, not everyone is going to have a passionate love for history. God has engineered each of us differently, called us to different pursuits, and equipped us with a specific passion for the unique ways in which we are to serve in his kingdom. This book is not intended to stir up a love of history within the reader. Rather, it is my desire to impart to the believer an awareness that history can and must be a meaningful part of his or her faith journey. In other words, the study of history can transform our faith. Conversely, in the following pages, I intend to present a theology of history that is a way of reading the human story with an eye for how it reveals and glorifies its divine author. Therefore, the twofold purpose of this book is to show how our view of the past enhances our faith and, in turn, how our faith informs our understanding of the past.

From the outset, it is necessary to form the distinction that I am speaking of history in this work in broad terms. Many contemporary Christians do possess a passionate interest in learning the history of the faith or studying biblical history as part of their regular study of scripture. Sacred history is important and, as we seek to learn and grow in our faith, it is imperative that we give attention to its historical development as well as the historical context in which the Bible was written. But while "biblical religion is historical"—and we must pay attention to this fact—scripture painstakingly reminds us that "the God of the Bible is pre-eminently the God of history."[3] Christ is Lord over *all* history, and "Christ is the meaning of history for Christians."[4] As we shall see in the coming pages, his glory is revealed as much through the events of so-called "secular" history as it is through the redemptive history that we find in the pages of scripture or the annals of church history to which we are now heirs. When we turn to history, whether we are talking about Moses parting the Red Sea, the Protestant Reformation, or the Cold War, we must read the story with eyes of faith, straining to perceive the ways in which God is revealing himself and advancing his kingdom in times of light and times of darkness.

The importance of history for the believer can be seen in the fact that God himself, far from creating the world and leaving it to its own designs, deigned to enter into history as a man. This again highlights not only the historical nature of our faith but also

3. Boice, *God and History*, 21.

4. Lewry, *Theology of History*, 59.

the impact that our faith brings to bear on our understanding of all of the historical process: "The inwardly historical character of Christ-formed grace and its power to shape history does not derive solely from the fact that Christ brings us the Father and reveals him through his earthly existence, his humanity becoming a living sacrament of the triune life, but from the fact that . . . he simultaneously assumed our history and tradition into himself."[5] God through Christ entered into the historical drama. What is more, this decisive event, this point on which history itself turns, enthrones Christ as the Lord of history. The entire story of mankind's existence, of empires and nations, plagues and famines, triumphs and tragedies, is the long tale of the outworking of God's kingdom inaugurated through Christ's first advent as we anticipate his return.

As Christians, the past beckons to us as God seeks to reveal himself in the human story. In the pages of sacred scripture, we find that "we read over and over again the words: 'Listen!', 'If you but listen to the voice of the Lord' . . . if you remain alert and attentive, you will hear something after all."[6] God is speaking to us through history, if only we are willing to listen. Through the annals of the past, we can behold the sovereignty of our God on display and rejoice in the unfolding of his kingdom plan for our redemption. History, then, leads us closer to God, reveals his nature to us, and gives us an assurance of his faithfulness to fulfill his plan for our redemption. We need only to listen, to yield ourselves to a christologically grounded appreciation of the past, and to stand in wonder at the workings of our savior—the Lord of history.

WHAT IS HISTORY?

One of the problems inhibiting Christians (and for that matter, anyone) from valuing the study of the past is the way in which history has traditionally been taught. Many find the subject to be

5. Balthasar, *Theology of History*, 75.

6. Haught, *Revelation*, 5.

daunting precisely because it has been presented in the same way as learning a foreign language. Students are encouraged to memorize facts, dates, and the names of long-dead kings and queens, without understanding with any real depth the world in which these bits of information gained meaning. This approach falls short. History should be about more than committing a list of facts to memory. I often encourage my students to refrain from focusing on the names and dates that I present to them and to instead focus on the broader story in which the historical drama unfolds.

But if history is not about memorization, then what is it? At the beginning of every class that I teach, I encourage my students to formulate a definition of history. On the surface, they believe that this is a relatively easy exercise: of course everyone knows what history is. But as they begin to submit their own definitions, they find that the question is more difficult than they first believed. Many offer the definition that history is anything that occurred in the past. I counter with the questions, "Is my waking up this morning a historical occurrence? My driving here? What I had for breakfast?" Students often then respond that there needs to be some component of importance behind what constitutes history, i.e., that history is everything that happened in the past that is also somehow meaningful. "What standards shall we use to determine what is meaningful?" I ask. "Who gets to sift through and decide what events are significant?" It is often remarked that history is written by the victors, and this is in many ways true. But does that mean that experiences that are not collectively regarded as "meaningful" do not constitute history? Are the stories of those left out of the historical narrative any less a part of history than those whose lives have entered the historical cannon? Some then submit that the existence of a written record provides a tenable criterion for a "meaningful" event and suggest we treat the existence of written evidence as the standard by which we admit an event into the category of "history." To be fair, the historical discipline is concerned primarily with texts (this is what distinguishes us from our archeologist colleagues, who are concerned primarily with artifacts), but this framework, too, falls short. What about societies that never developed a written language, but contributed to human development in other ways? Do these societies exist as a timeless Other, outside of the workings of that which we call history?

The problem here is that many of my students—and, I suspect, the American public in general—view history as an event or even a series of events. This again harkens back to how we have been taught history. If this were true, I would be willing to concede that history is merely an intellectual object, something to be explored only by the learned few. But categorizing history as an event falls short as an explanatory framework. History is much more than an event, or a series of events, for history is concerned with the ways in which events relate to one another. Most contemporary historians have adopted a simple definition of history that elevates it beyond rote recitation: history can be understood simply to be change over time. Historians study the processes by which human society has changed, whether they are focusing on political, economic, social, cultural, or any other form of history. They are interested in getting at how the human experience moved from point A to point B. As will be seen in the first chapter, they debate vociferously about how that change occurred and what the primary agents of that change are, but, for the most part, historians agree on the basic premise of the field as change over time.

When I use the term history in the coming pages, I am referring to this process of change over time. It is important that we understand this at the outset. If we fail to appreciate history for what it actually is, if we rely on popular perceptions, history will remain a meaningless quest for factoids, a dry set of lists of the names and dates that have somehow shaped our world without an actual appreciation of the ways in which they have done so. Every time you read the word history in this book, continually remind yourself of this definition, for it is crucial for understanding the thesis of this book.

Understanding history not as an endless string of dates and names allows us to better appreciate the present. The world in which we live, the things that are important in our society, and the challenges we face have been shaped by a process of change over time. Our world is not an accident nor has it sprung up *ex nihilo* from a vacuum. We are products of history, and we see the effects of history around us every day. When we read the headlines in the news, the stories that focus on war, terrorism, the sluggish economy, racial strife, and all the difficulties that beset us in our own time, we too often are drawn to frame these events in a presentist context. We ask what we can do to solve these issues now, but we fail to grasp the ways in which these circumstances came to be.

Historians are partially to blame for this. The past several decades of historical inquiry have privileged micro-histories that cover discrete, highly localized portions of the human story. The field of history has become increasingly esoteric and has lost sight of the bigger picture. Gone are the works of a past generation of historians that covered change over the *longue durée* (the long term), tracing historical change over the span of decades or centuries rather than focusing on a narrow time frame. We need to renew our interest in studying the larger fabric of the human story and to emphasize the ways in which change has occurred over a broad span of time. We need to restore our focus on understanding history as change over time if there is any chance of history becoming meaningful to a larger segment of the population. If we have any hope of seeing the ways in which an appreciation of the past can become meaningful for the believer, we must adopt this approach.[7]

WHY SHOULD CHRISTIANS ENGAGE THE PAST?

This book is divided into seven chapters, each of which reveals some way in which the study of history can and should be a meaningful exercise in the life of the believer or demonstrates how Christians and non-Christians understand the past differently.

---

7. A recent work by a pair of scholars has made just this point. Jo Guldi and David Armitage's *History Manifesto* issued a call to historians to begin to think again about history as a long-term process if there is to be any hope that history itself will become an agent of speaking truth to power in our contemporary times.

Each chapter can be read in isolation as an individual essay covering one aspect of Christian historical inquiry; however, it is best to read the chapters together in the order in which they are presented to gain a full picture of the ways in which the past can inform our faith. In particular, it is important to read the first two chapters first, as these provide an introductory framework illustrating the competing secular and Christian paradigms for assessing history.

The first chapter, "The Postmodern Paradigm of History: How the City of Man Understands its Past," explores postmodernism, the framework that currently dominates the field of history. Postmodernism submits that truth does not exist independent of human construction, countering the biblical worldview that truth can be located in God's self-revelation in the person of Christ. The purpose of the chapter is to set up that fact that history without God descends into a fruitless quest for humanity to produce its own meaning, independent of the divine. While there are things covered in the chapter that Christians can learn from a postmodern approach, in the end, we must reject postmodernism and postulate a Christian view of history.

The second chapter of the book, "He Removes Kings and Sets up Kings: The City of God's Understanding of the Past," sets about to formulate a Christian approach to the study of history. Taking a cue from Augustine's concept of the city of man and the city of God, I submit an alternative paradigm for Christians to approach the past that directly counters postmodernism's claim to the absolute subjectivity of truth. Two axioms are presented for developing a Christian theology of history. Firstly, we must consider Christ as the hermeneutic through which we read the events of the past. Secondly, we must counter postmodernism's distrust of truth and emphasis on the unknowability of the past with an assertion of God's sovereignty over the historical process. The second of these axioms in particular will be the guiding force throughout the rest of the book.

The third chapter, "Where was God in the Holocaust? The Narrative of History and the Question of Theodicy," sets about to tackle the obvious question that emerges when we submit God's absolute sovereignty over the historical process: If God is both sovereign *and*, as we can assume, good, why do horrific events like the Holocaust happen? As detailed in the chapter, there is no adequate philosophical or theological answer to this question. However, the chapter argues that history provides a narrative medium through which the question of theodicy can be addressed, providing the believer with a concrete space in which he or she can question God's goodness and sovereignty in faith. History, then, is meaningful for the believer in that it provides a channel through which we can engage some of the deepest questions of the faith.

The fourth chapter, "Heroes and Villains: The Lesson of History," flows from the third, posing the question as to whether or not there is a lesson Christians can learn from the past. Contrary to the oft-repeated sentiment that it is important to study history lest we repeat its mistakes, history does not provide a strictly practical lesson for ordering contemporary society to avoid revisiting our past failures. Rather, through using recent scholarly debates about the Holocaust as a case study, I propose that history provides a mirror through which the believer can see his or her own potential for sin. The past points us to our own depravity, calling us to challenge the sin that is present within us all. This, in turn, directs us toward our need of a savior and admonishes us to recognize the evil we permit in our own time.

Yet it is not enough to be left with a sense of our own sinfulness as we study the past, and the fifth chapter, "The Redemptive Value of the Past: Dealing with the Skeletons in our Closet," provides a framework through which history can call us to repentance. As citizens of nations, and as members of the Christian community, we must be willing to address the sins committed by our communities and the travesties committed in the name of our faith. We must counter narratives of history that ignore the darker episodes of our country's past and the less-than-savory aspects of church history. History becomes meaningful for believers in this context in that it calls us to confession and repentance at the national, ecclesial, and individual level and propels us to seek a cross-centered justice in the societies and time-frames in which we find ourselves.

The sixth chapter, "Militant Nostalgism: The Dangers of the Past," uncovers some of the ways in which an improper knowledge of the past warps our thinking in the present. There is a pervasive tendency in contemporary American society to long for the "simpler days" of the past. This desire is misguided, and it elides the very real problems that faced the periods of the past to which we long to return. Historical literacy provides a solution for this militant and misguided nostalgia and calls us to address the difficulties that beset our own times. Further, studying the past with an eye toward correcting the misplaced nostalgia of the present propels the believer toward a gospel-centered vision of time as embodied in the Christian practice of the liturgical year. Thus, history calls us to worship and to reconsider our own place within the divinely ordered historical drama.

The last chapter, "God and the End of History," challenges both the postmodern schematic that history has no end or logic and the popular globalist assumption that contemporary society represents the culmination of historical achievement. To establish a biblical framework to answer the question, "What/when is the end of history?" I draw a distinction between the end of history and the end of time, which are two separate, yet related, questions. I submit that to locate the end of history, we must not look to the end of the ages but rather to the incarnation of Christ, the Lord of history, whose kingdom was inaugurated at his birth, yet will not be fully realized until he comes again and subsumes the rise and fall of nations and empires, effectively resulting in the end of history. Equally important for the believer, however, as he or she considers the past, is the fact that the historical drama of which we are now participants will have a decisive and glorious end with Christ's return, as time itself draws to a close.

CONCLUSION

History thus has the power to enhance the believer's faith on a variety of levels. Through providing an avenue to address the difficult questions of our faith, a mirror through which we can see our own wickedness, a call to confession and repentance, a corrective to the idol of nostalgia, and a glimpse of the future that awaits us, the study of the past must become a part of every believer's life. This is a difficult task, for most Christians, as I have already admitted, do not possess a natural affinity for the subject. But there is much at stake here. More than just expanding our brains through a knowledge of the world that came before us, history can sanctify us, make us holy, and lead us to the Lord of history.

In this spirit, then, I invite you to consider the following chapters prayerfully. I challenge you to do the intellectual heavy-lifting that a Christian study of the past requires, to commit making history and historical awareness a fundamental part of your faith journey. Most of all, as we go on this journey together, I pray that you will see the Lord of history, the one who gives history meaning, the author of the human story. Though it is cliché to say, history is in fact his-story, and there is no greater benefit to a study of the past than to encounter Christ.

1

The Postmodern Paradigm of History: How the City of Man Understands its Past

"A Klee painting named 'Angelus Novus' shows an angel looking as though he is about to move away from something he is fixedly contemplating. His eyes are staring, his mouth is open, his wings are spread. This is how one pictures the angel of history. His face is turned toward the past. Where we perceive a chain of events, he sees one single catastrophe, which keeps piling wreckage upon wreckage and hurls it in front of his feet. The angel would like to stay, awaken the dead, and make whole what has been smashed. But a storm is blowing from Paradise; it has got caught in his wings with such violence that the angel can no longer close them. This storm irresistibly propels him into the future to which his back is turned, while the pile of debris before him grows skyward. This storm is what we call progress."[1]

"Pilate said to him, 'What is truth?'" (John 18:38)

---

1. Benjamin, *Philosophy of History*, 249.

AUGUSTINE, THE GREAT THINKER of the early church, conceived of two powers vying for domination in the world. He termed the two forces, which coexist in the temporal span of human history, "the city of man" and "the city of God." The former represents the kingdoms of this world as they rise and fall, never achieving the lasting glory for which they pine. The latter speaks of the heavenly city, the New Jerusalem, the culmination of the outworking of God's deliverance of his elect. Both cities compete for our loyalty, and both demand our worship. As believers, we must learn to order our lives as residents of the heavenly city while we, at least for a time, inhabit the city of man: our hearts can only belong to one or the other.

Augustine's bifurcated vision of the world can be seen in how human beings seek to uncover and understand their past. On the one hand, there is the city of man, which offers up understandings of history devoid of the divine. This is the angel of history imagined by social theorist Walter Benjamin, belayed as it were by the chaos laid at its feet as it pursues its vain resistance to the forces that would propel it into an equally chaotic future. The city of man's understanding of the past posits a nameless, impersonal storm mistakenly called progress as the author tasked with writing the human story. On the other hand, there is a Christian theology of history that reads the events of the past through the lens of God's sovereignty and his revelation of himself to mankind. In this vision, it is not the angel of history passively observing the human story unfold but rather a divine author who himself is committed to writing the story and revealing himself within it.

These two visions of the past are irreconcilable and are diametrically opposed to one another. The city of man's understanding of the past posits history as an unordered chaos, an accidental lurching forward of humanity as it is beset by circumstances that are not only beyond its control, but beyond any control. Here, history is a tragedy and when, as Benjamin conceives it, we misscategorize the march of time as progress, also an irony. In contrast, a Christian theology of history looks at the past and, through the apparent chaos, discerns, even if it cannot fully comprehend, a force guiding the pattern of human existence. What appears to be storms preventing the angel of history from gaining a sense of its own meaning is in fact a divine hand scripting the events of history as they unfold throughout the ages. What seems on the surface to be chaos is actually order.

In this chapter, we will explore the dominant analytical framework employed by the city of man to understand its past. This paradigm, which has come to dominate the professional study of history (though it still has its passionate detractors), is termed "postmodernism." It is this approach that dominates the history that most students encounter when taking courses at the university level. Further, the postmodern paradigm of history, like many other worldviews, has trickled from highbrow debates in academia into popular culture, becoming in the dominant way through which Americans perceive the world. Therefore, any meaningful discussion of a Christian theology of history, and of what Christians stand to gain through studying history, must begin by dissecting the opposite: a postmodern vision of the past, as represented by Benjamin's angel.

POSTMODERNISM AND THE SUBJECTIVITY OF TRUTH

In order to define postmodernism as it relates to historical inquiry, we first must establish what the term is not. Postmodernism has become a buzzword in the academy and in popular discourse, which has led to some confusion about its meaning. Many within the church remain wary of the word and, in their attempt to denounce its implications for Christians, have misscategorized it. Further, the label postmodernism has been applied in other disciplines in ways that do not explicitly relate to the ideas we are going to be discussing here. As an example, postmodern art describes a particular style and epoch of artistic production and does not, for the most part, relate to the postmodern theory that is relevant for our discussion.

Categorizing postmodernism is problematic. Postmodernism is not a religion. Indeed, there are Christian postmodernists (although, as will be seen when we discuss the central philosophies of postmodernism, it will hopefully be apparent that this term is something of a contradiction), Muslim postmodernists, Jewish postmodernists, atheist postmodernists, and so on. Postmodernism is also not by definition an ideology. One can derive an ideology from postmodernism, but studying the past through a postmodern lens does not automatically assume such an ideology. At its heart, postmodernism is not even a philosophy, although there is such a thing as postmodern philosophy.

What, then, is postmodernism? For the purposes of our discussion, we will focus on postmodernism as an analytical schema that historians employ to understand the past. Other disciplines—including (but not limited to) literary studies, philosophy, and other members of the humanities—also make use of the analytical framework of postmodernism in their work. Think of postmodernism as a set of tools, any one of which can be pulled out when a historian is conducting research. The tool is used to provide a framework through which to make sense of the world. As we saw in the introduction, historians define history as change over time, yet they fervidly argue as to how that change occurred. Postmodernism provides a set of answers for historians seeking to address how change happens. Noted British historian Callum Brown has summarized this well: "By not being an ideology, postmodernism is a way of understanding knowledge. It is a way of understanding how humans gain knowledge from the world."[2] Postmodernism is one among many analytic frameworks employed by historians, but over the last several decades has become ascendant.

The fundamental axiom of postmodernism is that all truth is subjective and therefore the product of human construction. Nineteenth-century philosopher Friedrich Nietzsche, considered by many to have laid the foundations of postmodern theory,

___

2. Brown, *Postmodernism for Historians*, 9. Brown's monograph is an excellent primer for understanding how postmodernism functions as a tool for historical analysis, though it comes from a secular perspective.

summarized this belief, proffering that, "There are no facts in themselves. It is always necessary to begin by introducing a meaning in order that there can be a fact."[3] For postmodernism, the "fact" itself is of no consequence and indeed does not exist independently. Facts are products of a process of "meaning-making," i.e., they come about as humans seek to articulate the world around them. This can be illustrated with an example. A postmodernist would make the claim that the floor beneath you does not exist. The designation "floor" is a product of human language and not a reality in and of itself. The "fact" of the floor, therefore, does not exist until we describe it with human vocabulary. Since the nuances of idioms vary from language to language, the floor exists differently as it is described by different persons in different languages in different historical situations. The designation "floor" exists only as we allow it to have semiotic meaning.

This approach is often incorrectly conflated with relativism, and the difference between relativism and postmodernism can be helpful in understanding how postmodernists conceive of the world. Relativism accepts different truths as equally valid. A relativist theology, for example, would maintain that there are multiple paths to God; no one religion can claim to be an absolute truth, and indeed multiple religions could simultaneously be true. Postmodernism avoids assessing the validity of truth altogether. Postmodernism posits that all that which we call "truth" is in fact only true because we have designated it as such. There is no one truth that is "true," nor are multiple truths simultaneously "true." Truth is in the eye of the beholder as defined by his or her specific location in time and space.

At this point, before we have even gotten into the weeds of postmodern theory or applied it to our understanding of the past, we can begin to see the contradictions between a postmodern worldview and a Christian one. Christianity posits the existence of an immutable truth that can be located in the divine. This truth, contrary to the postmodern assumption, *exists*; it is unchanging, unchallenged, and unconditioned by human interpretation. This

3. Cited in Brown, *Postmodernism*, 4.

truth finds its fullest expression in the person of Jesus Christ, God's ultimate revelation of truth to the world. For the Christian, what constitutes truth is not up for debate. For the postmodernist, the very category of truth itself is fictive.

POSTMODERNISM, POWER, AND THE HISTORICAL PROCESS

The whole of postmodern theory flows from the axiom that truth exists only to the extent that we create it and give it meaning. To understand the assumptions that flow from this, and then to see how these assumptions apply specifically to the historical discipline, we can begin by tracing the historical forces that shaped the development of postmodern theory. Postmodernism emerged as a challenge to the modernist worldview that preached a teleological view of history as an unmitigated march of progress. Modernists saw the advancements in science and industry in the late-nineteenth and early twentieth centuries as the triumph of human intellect over the forces of nature and believed that humanity was on a permanent upward trajectory that would result in universal peace and prosperity. Within the church, modernist theologians saw the start of the twentieth century as the dawning of the prophesied millennium in which human achievement would bring the perfection of Christ's kingdom to earth.

These idealistic views were shattered with the twin catastrophes of the world wars, which saw technology and nationalism—the idols of the modernist worldview—bring about the death of tens of millions for seemingly no cause. In the philosophical void that followed the world wars, intellectuals began to challenge the tenets of modernism together with traditional sources of power within society, such as religious and state institutions, and sought a new paradigm of knowledge. Simultaneously, the first half of the twentieth century saw the rise of social movements, such as the first wave of the feminist movement, which began to subvert the existing power structures cherished by modernism. Cultural works, such as Joseph Conrad's *Heart of Darkness*, a compelling novel that belied the myth of Belgium's supposedly "benevolent" colonialism in the Congo, brought these critiques to popular culture. With these challenges to the mechanisms of authority that modernists held dear and the devastation brought about by the world wars, postmodern theory came into being, though it would not be until the last two decades of the century that it would be embraced by historians.

This brief sketch outlines a fundamental aspect of postmodern theory. In addition to the axiomatic assumption that truth is subjective and that reality, as a result, is fundamentally unknowable, postmodern theory emphasizes the interplay between truth and power. French philosopher Michel Foucault (1926–1984), a towering figure in postmodern thought, articulated a theory of knowledge-power in which truth is created primarily as a mechanism of power. Foucault posited that societies joined different "facts" together to create what is termed a discourse, and that discourse, in turn, empowered certain groups within society. Foucault maintained that discourse is productive. Categories such as "homosexual," he argued, were figments of the human imagination, a tool in a quest to establish a patriarchal regime. He stressed that prior to the late-nineteenth century, when much of the understandings we have today about sexuality began to be codified, homosexuals did not "exist." He acknowledged that certainly there were men who had sexual relations with men, and women who had sexual relations with women, but that it was not until the nineteenth century that western society chose to attach the label "homosexual" to such behaviors, thus, in effect, creating the category "homosexual" as a fact.[4] Here it may be helpful to remember the floor example: the floor does not exist as a fact until we chose to subjectively describe it as such. For Foucault, homosexuality was a created concept, one inexorably linked to power.

The relationship between the postmodern axiom that facts do not exist until we create them and power cannot be overstressed. Power is at the heart of the postmodern paradigm, and power is established through the creation of knowledge. Postmodern

4. See Foucault, *History of Sexuality*.

theorists maintain that many of the accepted categories cherished by modernism—race, class, gender, sexuality, nationality, etc.—were not only invented truths but also established in the context of power relations.

Two other examples are instructive of how this process works and how postmodern theory can be applied to historical inquiry. The category of "race" was central to a modernist understanding of the world. In the late nineteenth century, modernist thinkers in the United States believed that there was a fundamental difference between an individual with darker skin and an individual with lighter skin. To the modernist, "race" as a category was an immutable truth, an *a priori* fact grounded in scientific objectivism, much like gravity. However, postmodernism claims all truth to be subjective. Therefore, a postmodernist historian understands the category "race" to be unstable. Different notions of what constitutes race (it should come as no surprise that race is defined differently, for example, in France versus the United States, or even in the contemporary United States versus the nineteenth-century United States) evolved in the context of struggles over power. Certainly postmodernist thinkers understand that there are a variety of different shades of human skin; however, they define race as the process through which those differences gained cultural relevancy and meaning in the context of power struggles. Specifically, postmodern scholars understand race to be a product of the transatlantic slave trade, where the category "black" developed as a means for legitimizing a system that was economically beneficial to those who belonged to the category "white."

Similarly, postmodernists see "gender" as an unstable category whose definition shifts in societies across time and space. For postmodernists, gender, like race, is *not* an *a priori* fact of nature. Rather, gender is an invention of human society. A postmodernist would *not* deny that there are physical differences (genitalia, chromosomes, etc.) between those classified as "men" and those classified as "women," any more than in our example about the non-existence of the floor one would deny that something separates the thinker from the ground. However, in addition to pointing to the aberrations that exist from those norms (indeterminate genitalia, alternative chromosomal arrangements, etc.), postmodernists maintain that the fact of gender, the ascription of identities based on physiological difference, is a product of language and culture. Prominent historian of France Joan Wallach Scott synthesized this thought well in her seminal monograph on the use of gender for understanding history, defining gender as "knowledge about sexual difference," with knowledge being used in the Foucauldian sense of knowledge-power discussed above.[5]

Both examples show how postmodern theory works out in interpretive practice, providing an inchoate picture of the impact of postmodernism on historical inquiry. In the development of the categories "race" and "gender," there is a basic progression that illustrates how postmodernism understands the "development" of truth. Meaning is attached to objects of benign significance within the physical or human world, and, as these meanings are strung together, they constitute what postmodernism terms "discourse." Race is a discourse (actually, many discourses working together in a matrix of power), as is gender. Other categories such as nation, class, and ethnicity, also function similarly.

THE IMPACT OF POSTMODERNISM ON THE HISTORICAL DISCIPLINE

In the mid-twentieth century, the discipline of history was caught in a rut for decades. A British historian I know once lamented that every dissertation written in Great Britain during the 1970s was titled "The Impact of the Industrial Revolution on _____," where each student studied the impact of the Industrial Revolution on a small town in England to reach essentially the same conclusion with different names. The linguistic turn, the term used by scholars to denote the growing impact of postmodernism on historical inquiry starting roughly in the 1980s, transformed history, resulting in an explosion of new histories being written.

5. Scott, *Gender*, 2.

To be clear, aspects of the linguistic turn have had a positive effect on history as well. Postmodernism has led to a shift from exclusively writing histories of the powerful to considering the perspectives of the marginalized. This is, without any qualifications, a positive development (we will discuss this further in the third chapter). Further, postmodernism's emphasis on power dynamics has elevated identity as a category of analysis for historians, leading to a rich historiography on identity that has been invaluable not only to our understandings of the past but also to addressing questions of injustice in the present (more on this in chapter 5).

While postmodernism has had positive impacts on the historical discipline over the last three decades, an absolute embrace of the worldview it offers leads to a hollow understanding of the past. Prominent historian Hayden White's seminal work, *Metahistory: The Historical Imagination in Nineteenth Century Europe*, exemplifies this. In *Metahistory*, White submits that the work of the historian is suspiciously similar to that of the novelist. White identities four literary genres—romance, tragedy, comedy, and satire—in which historians write, arguing that historians are crafting a narrative much in the way that an author writes a novel.[6] To be sure, White and other postmodern historians hold to certain standards of disciplinary objectivity and distinguish history from fiction through historians' basis in archival study and the peer-review process. However, seeing history through the lens of genre leads to a philosophy of history that posits the past as unknowable and, in stronger terms, meaningless outside of the context of the present. In this formulation, the past is not a reality itself that the historian seeks to uncover (as a scientist would uncover the laws of the universe) but rather a field through which meaning is produced by the historian as she or he writes it into being. A postmodern analysis suggests that historians make their object, i.e., create the very subject they study. This flatly contradicts a Christian worldview that posits an eternal God, existing outside of the parameters of time and space, yet intervening into those parameters to make himself known. For the Christian, the past happened, and what is more,

---

6. See White, *Metahistory*.

God has deigned to reveal himself through that past to those of us who live in the present.

As Christians coming to the past to form and shape our faith, we must be aware of the dangers presented by postmodernism. We confess the existence of truth, denying the core of postmodern analysis. We accept the knowability of the past, challenging White's blurring of the lines between factual historical writing and fiction. It is critical that we know the dangers of a postmodernist interpretation of the past. At the same time, we must also acknowledge that postmodernism has contributed some value to the study of the past, even as we reject its central tenets. While the postmodernist claims to the unknowability of reality and subjectivity of truth are contradictory to biblical Christianity, Christians can and must acknowledge that, while there is fundamental truth, and while God has intentionally and clearly revealed that truth (including through the historical process), there are aspects of contemporary society that are accepted as truth that we must reject. As an example, the historical development of the categories of "race," "gender," and "sexuality" discussed in the previous section *are* compelling arguments, and I am comfortable asserting their validity. We must, however, be careful not to give ourselves over to a postmodern worldview that stipulates that *every* truth is created, that the angel of history is being blown by an unknowable force, and that humanity itself defines reality. This requires discernment, but appreciating this nuance is an important step toward embracing a Christian theology of history in a world bent on promoting a postmodern understanding of the past.[7]

An example of applying aspects of postmodern interpretation of the past while rejecting the absolute subjectivity of truth can be found in the case of the development of the concept of race in the United States. As discussed above, most scholars argue that race is not a biological reality (i.e., a "truth") but rather developed

---

7. Here, the analogy of postmodernism as a belt of tools for analyzing the past is helpful, for the Christian historian may select from those tools from time to time—to aid in his or her analysis, when appropriate—without claiming the entire belt.

conceptually as a discourse to legitimize slavery. Such an analysis rests on the tools provided by postmodernism. It takes a "fact" and deconstructs its a *priori* existence by tracing its development across time and space. This is a reading of the past that I concur with. However, I would wish to see this thesis carried further. A number of other historians and I find credible the argument that the American Civil War was caused by slavery. This is a claim that asserts an absolute truth, which postmodernism forbids. What is more, this truth carries with it a moral dimension, for it is laden with implications for the development of the concept of race and the position of race in the United States in a manner that impacts contemporary society. Thus, while I am willing to borrow from postmodern analysis the idea that *certain* truths in society—in this case, race—are in fact subjective, I am not willing to champion the idea that *all* truth is. Again, this requires great discernment.

Just as Augustine argued that we must learn to temporarily dwell in the city of man and to seek its good even as we remain grounded in our identity as citizens of the city of God, the task of the Christian, as she or he engages the past, is to take what is of value in the city of man's approach to history and to fit it into a christological framework. In other words, we can learn methodology, analysis, and narrative from our postmodern counterparts but *must* reject postmodernism as the lens through which we view the past. Rather, as we will do in the next chapter, we must develop a Christian theology of history that submits the person of Christ (i.e., the perfect revelation of God) and God's total sovereignty over history as our axiom to counter postmodernism's rejection of truth. To have a full, God-formed view of the past, we must view truth as a person, eternal in existence, immutable in character.

HISTORY, POSTMODERNISM, AND MORALITY

The task of the historian necessarily involves engaging questions of morality. As a historian of the contemporary Middle East, I have found that most of my colleagues developed a moral perspective on some question facing the region before engaging its history (for example, taking a position on the Palestine conflict), and have sought to frame their work, at least implicitly, along the lines of that moral basis. But morality is also in the background of those who study more benign histories (such as, for instance, a historian I met who studies sixteenth-century Swedish intellectual history). As we will see in the next chapter, history is a vehicle of God's revelation, one of a myriad of ways in which he reveals his person and character to us. History, therefore, has a way of shaping our moral horizons. For the Christian, history and morality are fundamentally linked.[8] As we look at postmodernism's impact on the historical discipline, it is necessary to take a brief detour and consider the implications of postmodern historical inquiry for moral thought.

Postmodernism's impact on morality stems from its denial of objective truth. Brown has stated that postmodernism "argues that morality comes from *a sense of the immoral.* . . . Immoralities are declared, not proven. . . . The decision as to what is acceptable behavior and what is not acceptable behavior has to be taken by each generation, and by each person within each generation."[9] Thus, for the postmodernist, murder is wrong because society has collectively agreed murder is wrong. Without the subjective analysis of culture, the act of taking another human's life is neither "good" nor "bad," for such categories are the product of human convention. Clearly, this colors a postmodern view of the past. How are we to understand the horrors of the Holocaust, to which a majority of German citizens attached a positive, moral value? Should we concur with their judgment or apply a moral code based in our own context to condemn such acts of evil? If we assume a postmodern position, we can condemn the evil of race-based slavery in the United States based on the conventions we have adopted here, in the present, but can we judge those who went before us who operated under a different moral framework?

8. I am not suggesting a modernist conception of history as moral teacher, whereby we ascertain right and wrong through the examples of our foremothers and forefathers. Rather, I am referring here to God's self-revelation through the created order, including the human story. This will hopefully become clearer as the book progresses.

9. Brown, *Postmodernism*, 144–45.

Postmodern approaches to history negate the reality of a world marred by sin. Indeed, the very category of "sin" is anathema to postmodern thought. For postmodernists, the concept of right and wrong are products of historical and societal discourse, not immutable truths. Postmodernists *do* see a role for morality in society, though they locate the "truth" from which that morality springs as a dynamic consensus reached by society. Something is moral if society (or even an individual) has deemed it as such. Such a definition, as it has reached the public perception, has led to a confused notion of morality based on feelings—a morality that changes with the times and is subject to no higher law. In such a conception, the categories of right and wrong lose meaning, and persons are free to determine for themselves what is right.

For the Christian, morality is rooted in both the revealed word of a knowable God, through scripture, and especially though the incarnation of Christ. Morality, therefore, is rooted neither in an objective application of the lessons of the past, as modernist historians of a past era would have it, nor epistemologically derived by applying prevailing constructed social norms, as postmodern historians would have it. Morality exists *a priori* as an outflow of the very nature of the God who exists outside the parameters of time and historical development. Our belief about truth matters to historical inquiry. Is truth derived subjectively, as the storm blows the angel of history along? Or is there a transcendent source of truth behind that storm? Only when we insert the objective "who" of morality into historical discourse will we begin to grasp how studying the past can transform our faith.

CONCLUSION

In the end, postmodernism produces a hollow understanding of the past. The progress of Benjamin's angel is driven by an unknowable force, a collection of subjective truths divorced from a concrete reality. For historical inquiry to make sense, the past must not only be knowable but also must be grounded in reality. Consider, for instance, how a postmodern worldview would impact our understanding of race relations in the Jim Crow era. Were the untold sufferings of black Americans merely a fashioned narrative? Does not a postmodern worldview deconstruct their experiences into oblivion? Can we fashion a moral critique of white America in the face of such travesties if we accept a postmodern moral system? At stake in the impact of postmodernism on historical inquiry are actual human experiences with contemporary political ramifications. As Christians, we believe that humans are created in the image of God. Postmodernism, through rejecting an abject reality of experience, tarnishes and denies that image.

Therefore, we are left at the point of needing a decidedly Christian theology of history, which we will begin to develop in the next chapter. Postmodernism falters in that it rejects the Christian claim that truth can be located in the person of Christ. History without Christ as its hermeneutic fails, for "without Christ, philosophies of history tend either to embrace a religion of progress towards an earthly utopia or to relapse into the absurdity of rise and decline of successes which always end in failure; without hope in Christ, attempts to systematize history end in presumption or despair about the goal of history."[10] Christians cannot leave Benjamin's angel to falter on its own against the storm of chaos and call it progress; rather, we must discover the Lord of the storm in the midst of the chaos. From that point, Christ will transform our reading of the past, and humanity's story will lead us to Christ.

10. Lewry, *Theology of History*, 80.

2

He Removes Kings and Sets up Kings: The City of God's Understanding of the Past

"The goal of history is the one intended by God, and he brings it to this end in the accomplishment of his plan for salvation. God is the Lord of History, and his sovereignty has been made known to the Christian in Christ."[1]

"Any attempt to interpret history as a whole, if it is not to succumb to gnostic myth, must post some subject which works in and reveals itself in the whole of history and which is at the same time a being capable of providing general norms. This can only be either God himself . . . or man."[2]

"He changes times and seasons; he removes kings and sets up kings; he gives wisdom to the wise, and knowledge to those who have understanding; he reveals deep and hidden things; he knows what is in the darkness, and the light dwells with him." (Dan 2:21–22)

---

1. Lewry, *Theology of History*, 58–59.
2. Balthasar, *Theology of History*, 11–12.

J. R. R. TOLKIEN's masterful trilogy, *The Lord of the Rings*, provides more than a riveting tale and artful prose for the reader. As a most unlikely hero journeys through Middle Earth, making a last stand against the forces of evil assailing a world of great beauty, Tolkien's pen endeavors to impart a series of lessons. The one Ring cautions about the corrupting nature of power and how difficult an idol it can be to let go. The yield to temptation by Boromir, followed by his tragic passing, paints a beautiful picture of redemption even for one who has fallen so fast from so far a height, echoing Peter's denial before Christ's crucifixion, subsequent restoration, and redemption. Tolkien pictures humanity as both weak and strong, given to bouts of rage and temptation that lead to self-destruction, yet also prone to wisdom and valor.

From one of Tolkien's darkest and most tragic characters— the creature Gollum—the reader catches a glimpse of the ways in which faith frames our understanding of the past. Gollum began his life as Smeagol, a simple Hobbit. A shadow was forever cast over his life when, by chance, his friend Deagol discovered the Ring of power, whereafter passion overtook poor Smeagol, who, in his craven lust for the power that the Ring promises, killed his friend. Smeagol fled to the mountains, where he spent generations admiring the token that became the sole object of his worship, even as his body was corrupted and warped by the evil of the Ring.

By what appears to an imperceptive reader to be chance, Gollum lost the Ring to Bilbo Baggins, setting the stage for the eventual journey on the part of Bilbo's nephew, Frodo, to destroy it. The telling point of Gollum's role in the plot came as Frodo suggested to the wise wizard Gandalf that things would have been much better had Bilbo simply killed Gollum when he had the chance, for Gollum posed a grave threat to Frodo's mission. Gandalf submitted that such an action would not have only been immoral but shortsighted as well. Turning to the hobbit, the wizard sagaciously remarked:

> Deserves it! I daresay he does. Many that live deserve
> death. And some that die deserve life. Can you give it
> to them? Then do not be too eager to deal out death in

judgment. For even the very wise cannot see all ends. I
have not much hope that Gollum can be cured before he
dies. . . . My heart tells me that he has some part to play
yet, for good or ill, before the end; and when that comes,
the pity of Bilbo may rule the fate of many.[3]

In this one deft remark, Gandalf not only issued a warning about
the dangers of rushing to mete out judgment but also articulated
a biblical theology of history that counters the postmodern vision
of the previous chapter.

The key to understanding Gandalf's wisdom is the phrase:
"For even the wise cannot see all ends." In spite of Gandalf's hope,
Gollum was never reformed. But that didn't mean that he faded
from the story. Rather, he was the instrument that led Frodo into
the very heart of Mount Doom, the only location where the Ring
could be destroyed. As Frodo stood on a precipice before the fire
at the heart of the mountain, his goodness wavered, and he chose
to claim the Ring for himself rather than cast it into the flame. The
promised deliverance seemed to falter. Yet from the shadows crept
a dark, twisted figure who desired to reclaim the Ring for himself.
Gollum attacked Frodo, and, in their scuffle, Gollum and the Ring
plummeted into the fire. The Ring was consumed, and Middle
Earth was delivered from its darkness.

What is at work here is remarkable. Together with Gandalf,
the reader desires greatly for Gollum's redemption. We all love a
conversion story. But that is not to be Gollum's fate. Yet in spite
of his wickedness, regardless of the fact that, even in the end, he
sought the Ring for his own ends, Gollum becomes an instrument
of deliverance. Elsewhere in his conversation with Frodo, Gandalf
belied an unseen hand working for good in the tragic tale of Gollum's life: "Behind [Bilbo's discovery of the Ring] there was something else at work, beyond any design of the Ring-maker. I can put
it no plainer than by saying that Bilbo was *meant* to find the Ring,
and *not* by its maker. In which case you were *meant* to have it.
And that may be an encouraging thought."[4] This unseen force that

3. Tolkien, *Lord of the Rings*, 65.
4. Tolkien, *Lord of the Rings*, 61.

works through Gollum's wickedness is that which gives meaning to the chaos encountered by the angel of history. Behind the storm that endlessly propels the angel toward the future, working in the chaos of a disintegrating reality, is the steady hand of the Lord of history, directing all—whether good or evil—for his glory.

THE AXIOM OF CHRISTIAN HISTORY: THE SOVEREIGNTY OF GOD

In the previous chapter, we traced how secular historians frame the past through the lens of postmodernism. Postmodernism claims that truth does not exist *a priori* but rather is developed subjectively by those who claim it. This postulates a past that is chaotic, subject to the whims of those who wish to understand it. History in this scheme is about humanity making its own meaning.

In this chapter, it is our task to reach the counter of this proposal, a history that is grounded in a preexisting truth based on divine self-revelation. We will begin by asserting a counter-claim to the postmodern axiom that truth is subjective. Here it is not enough to merely submit that truth exists objectively; numerous religions and philosophies exist that would also make this claim. Indeed, the humanist-centered historical modernism, postmodernism's antecedent, accepted the existence of objective truth. Rather, we must postulate an alternative axiom that challenges postmodern interpretations of the truth by grounding that truth not in philosophy, theory, religion, or a specific text, but in the person of Christ. For Christians, then, Christ becomes our hermeneutic for reading the past.

A christological reading of history presupposes divine lordship over the human experience, for Christ came as king. Therefore, the axiom from which a Christian theology of history flows is that God is the center of history and retains absolute sovereignty over the totality of history. By this I mean that every event of history, from the minutia of my waking up this morning, to the rise and fall of nations, to the darkest events of history such as the Holocaust, are ordained and authored by God for his own glory.

In this schema, God is not merely the one who allows history to happen and then reacts to human agency but rather *is* the agency himself. The actions of humans, whether wicked or righteous, are written on the pages of history by the divine author who alone knows the end of the tale.

No better understanding of God's sovereignty over the historical process can be found than in the accounts of the Hebrew prophets. Elisha and his servant caught a glimpse of the unseen forces of God behind the historical drama. As the king of Syria sought to capture the prophet (who kept foiling his plans to attack Israel through revealing the movements of the king's troops), Elisha and his servant found themselves surrounded by the Syrian host. Fearful, the servant cried out. In response, Elisha prayed that the man's eyes would be open to perceive God's intervention, and the servant saw the great host of heaven surrounding the army of the Syrians (2 Kgs 8:6–23). This episode magnifies the hidden yet sure sovereignty of God. History plays out neither on the strength of the armies of Syria nor on any other geopolitical reality but rather on the steadfast decree of the divine sovereign whose host cements his lordship over the historical process. A little later in Israel's history, the prophet Habakkuk wrote about the coming onslaught of God's people by the Babylonians, admonishing Israel to "Look among the nations, and see; wonder and be astounded, for I am doing a work in your days that you would not believe if told. For behold, I am raising up the Chaldeans, that bitter and hasty nation" (Hab 1:5–6a). Here, and through the rest of the book, we see that God executes his sovereignty even through the actions of evil men. God raised up wicked Babylon as an instrument of his judgment. Finally, we can turn to the book of Daniel, which recounts the prophet's service to successive kings of Babylon and Persia. Daniel's entire prophecy centers on God revealing to his people that his hand is behind the raising up and removal of kings and empires, all of which are to be subsumed under the coming rule of God's kingdom found in Christ.

The New Testament similarly reveals the powerful workings of God through the historical process. The birth of our eternal king, the Lord of history, was brought about by God's ordering of the historical process. Jesus' parents were from Nazareth, yet the scripture proclaimed that he was to be born in Bethlehem (Mic 5:2). Through a decree of Caesar Augustus, Joseph and Mary were required to travel to Bethlehem at the time of the divine birth. Though Augustus did not perceive it, the emperor's census fit into the divine plan. God wields the hearts even of those rulers who know nothing of him in order to actualize his purposes. The book of Acts chronicles the growth of the church in historical perspective and demonstrates God's sovereignty over the most hopeless of circumstances. As he ascended into heaven, Christ commanded the disciples to take his message to the ends of the earth. Yet at the start of Acts, we find them locked in the upper room (Acts 1:8). God brought about a persecution of the early church in Jerusalem that forced his people into exile throughout the Roman Empire, thus carrying the message with them (Acts 8:1). The despair of persecution was an instrument of God to call all nations to himself. In the book of Revelation, we see time and again God's powerful working in human history to expand his kingdom through the growth of his church. Every force that seems bent on the destruction of God's people is in fact under divine rule and guidance.[5]

The notion of God's absolute sovereignty over history is a thoroughly biblical one, and thus the paradigm we as Christians should adopt as we seek to engage the past. God raises up and brings down peasants and kings, nations and empires, all working for his purposes. He has deigned to enter the human drama to reveal himself to us, to bring about our redemption, out of concern and love for his creation, and a zeal for his own glory. We do not serve a God that is far off, a God that creates and then forgets. Rather, we serve a God who adamantly wants to be a part of his creation, a God whose passion for his own glory forces him into the historical process. To have a faith-formed appreciation of history is to delight in the sovereignty of God, to know that he is

---

5. One of many examples would be John's vision of the sixth angel (Rev 16:12–14), where God issued the decree for the unclean spirits to precede forth in order to accomplish his purposes within human events.

advancing his kingdom through light and darkness. It shifts our perspectives to the eternal as we acknowledge his lordship in the darkest days of human life, rejoicing in divine purposes. It drives us to see our own ephemeral nature, causing us to look to the things that are above. Yet at the same time, it keeps us grounded, ready to be agents of God's kingdom in the here-and-now. History draws us to remember our own salvation, and to behold it as part of God's ongoing program of redemption.

From this we can begin to see what a Christian theology of history looks like. In contrast to Benjamin's angel of history, a Christian theology of history centers on the divine as the chief and total force driving time. Though we share with Benjamin (and also the preacher in Ecclesiastes) a sense that humanity cannot advance its own destiny, when we acknowledge the absolute sovereignty of God, and when we couple that doctrine with an unswerving belief in his innate goodness, we begin to see that the perceptively unordered chaos of the human experience indeed has a script: the will of God. We may not know the *why* of the events, but we can rest in confidence and awe at knowing the *who*.

As we locate the logic of history within the paradigm of divine sovereignty, we are in a position to challenge postmodernism's assertion of the subjectivity of truth. If God is the center, purpose, and agent of history, and if truth finds its origin in the divine, then truth exists outside of the human capacity to create it. What is more, God's truth does not change, for his character does not change (Heb 13:8). Truth does not enter the world through the constructs of man. Truth is the practical overflow of the holy nature of God. This truth finds its fullest expression in God's ultimate revelation of himself to us in history through the person of Christ. Thus the ultimate event of history, the incarnation—an event that Christians regard as truth—was God's embodiment of truth itself.

This is of utmost importance for our engagement with history in that it challenges postmodernism's schematic of the unknowability of the past. Rather than seeing the strident flow of history as an unmitigated chaos, Christians see the deliberate interventions of a God who seeks to make himself known through the historical process. Berkovits summarizes this interplay between sovereignty and revelation well, and is worth quoting at length:

> The foundation of religion is not the affirmation that God *is*, but that God is concerned with man and the world; that, having created this world, he has not abandoned it, leaving it to its own devices; that he cares about his creation. It is the essence of biblical religion that God is sufficiently concerned about man to address him; and that God values man enough to render himself approachable by him. In the Bible, God and man face each other, as it were. God wants something of man, and man may entreat God. . . . Biblical religion bases itself on the possibility of a relationship between God and man.[6]

Thus, God's revelation of himself through the historical process, his pernicious refusal to leave man to his own devices, points us to our need for relationship with him. As we study history, then, we should be led toward that relationship.

GOD'S SOVEREIGNTY IN THE RUTH NARRATIVE

Having now provided a basic sketch of a Christian theology of history, we can turn to one of the most powerful narrative accounts in scripture, the story of Ruth, to begin to see the different ways in which God exercises his sovereignty over the historical process. God commands creation to orchestrate his plans, works through righteous individuals to bring redemption to his people, orders the actions of the wicked to bring about good for his people, and raises up the wicked for judgment against his people.

If there ever was an unlikely candidate for someone who would change the entire trajectory of human history, it was Ruth. A Moabite, Ruth was an outsider to God's chosen people of Israel. What is more, her marriage to an Israelite came about through the darkest of circumstances. Her father-in-law, Elimelech, lived in the promised land with his wife Naomi. When famine struck the land, Elimelech and Naomi were faced with a choice. God had

6. Berkovits, *God, Man, and History*, 15.

commanded his people to dwell in the land of promise, yet as the land failed to produce, the two had to decide between obedience to the divine decree and certain starvation.

Naomi and Elimelech fled to the neighboring country of Moab. Moab serves in the Old Testament as the arch opposite of God's rule. It was a land of idolatry, full of a people who practiced injustice. Yet in their desperate flight of disobedience, this is where Elimelech and Naomi chose to sojourn. Life became comfortable again, and the couple had two sons. In time, each son took a wife from among the women of Moab: one married Ruth and another married Orpah. Elimelech and Naomi rested in the hope that God was choosing to bless them outside of the land of blessing. Tragedy returned to the house when Elimelech and his two sons died, leaving Naomi, Ruth, and Orpah without support in a patriarchal society. In her despondence, Naomi released Ruth and Orpah to return to their families to secure a new future. Orpah took the offer. Ruth passionately refused, tying her fate to that of Naomi, choosing to adopt her mother-in-law's people and God as her own.

The great reversal that comes next is familiar territory for most Christians. Upon their return to Bethlehem, Ruth meets her kinsman Boaz while gleaning grain in his field. Through Naomi's wisdom, Boaz redeems Ruth. Ruth is blessed with children, reestablishing Elimelech's line and heritage. One of her descendants, David, became Israel's greatest king. Even further down the line, a greater descendent was born; the king who would rule all other kings, the very son of God, the Lord of history.

Our Sunday morning sermons tend to trivialize the story of Ruth by focusing on the young woman from Moab as the main character of the story. Yet if we read deeper, we find that this story is not about Ruth at all. Nor is it about Elimelech, Naomi, Orpah, or Boaz. It is not even, as some commentators suggest, a means of introducing King David. Rather, the book extols the glory of God as he intervenes in many powerful ways in human history to accomplish his purposes. As such, it provides an excellent text for developing a Christian theology of history.

Nestled within the Ruth story is an oft overlooked detail that magnifies God's providence over the historical process. Ruth's entrance into the story was brought about not by human ingenuity but rather God working through the created order to set into motion the establishment of the Davidic line that would culminate in the birth of Christ. The geographically localized famine that struck Israel at this point in the period of the judges compelled Elimelech to disobey the covenantal command of dwelling in the land in order to sojourn among Israel's hated neighbors, the Moabites. Without the famine, Elimelech's son would have never wed Ruth, and the divine plan for raising up a deliver for Israel would have faltered. Yet, in his providence, God sent the famine.

Do you see what is at work here? The God who created the heavens and the earth, the Lord over all, commanded his creation to bring devastation on his own people. What at the time caused death, destruction, and despair, was in fact the outworking of the divine plan that would transform the world. God's intervention through the famine was what brought Ruth into God's program of redemption. This Moabite woman, destined by geography and genealogy to live outside of God's chosen community of grace, was brought to salvation through God's work in the historical process. But God's plans were for more than just Ruth. Through the connection she established with Naomi, the Davidic line was established, and from that line would spring the one on whom all human history would turn: the Messiah, the king of kings, the one who came not just to deliver the nation of Israel, but who would open the door of salvation to all. All of this was brought to fruition through the sovereignty of God in the famine, a chain of consequences unbeknownst to the characters in the story. This is how God works in history: in ways unknown to us, through circumstances that at the time may seem to signal defeat for his people, yet ultimately serve for his own glory and our deliverance. Thus, when we look at history and see famines, earthquakes, and plagues, we may not, in our human frailty, be able to ascertain with certainty what exactly the divine plan is, yet we can rest assured and rejoice in the sovereignty of God.

The characters in the Ruth story also reveal how God's agency works through human actors in the historical process. Ruth's faithfulness achieved the outworking of the divine plan. Judged by the standards of her day, Ruth was of no consequence; a gentile living outside of God's redeemed community. Yet God chose precisely this person to accomplish his will. Ruth's steadfast determination to remain with Naomi was a gift of a gracious God, and without this gift the story would have fallen apart. Often, God will raise up righteous men and women to accomplish his program of redemption in the historical process. Sometimes God works through such persons to achieve national deliverance, as was the case with Deborah (Judg 5), and sometimes God raises up the righteous to achieve spiritual deliverance, as was the case with Ruth and, later in the scripture, Mary. God frequently does use his servants in the historical process to build his kingdom in the here and now. History is littered with the testimony of women and men of faith who led their people to deliverance in national terms (one can think here of the many faith leaders who were instrumental in the Civil Rights Movement in America) or in the spiritual realm (such as the countless men and women of God throughout the ages who have brought about revival in the church and evangelistic movements throughout the world).

We must, however, be cautious when we encounter these individuals in history. Too often, Christians lionize such persons, placing them on the pedestal of their own agency. We need to remind ourselves that Ruth was not the main character of her own narrative. Rather, in God's grace and sovereignty, and through his own agency, Ruth became a divine ambassador set in place to accomplish the purposes of God. We must stay our hearts from transferring our worship and trust from God to his servants, remembering that "just because God deploys human ambition doesn't mean he condones human arrogance. Being used by God does not exempt anyone from humility before God."[7] When we look to the past and see great men and women of God accomplishing wonderful things for the kingdom, we should not revel in their skill, accomplish-

7. Ortlund, *Isaiah*, 107.

ments, or tenacity but rather rejoice in the awesome sovereignty of God as he raises up the righteous for his glory.

Not every character in the Ruth story exemplified the same laudable characteristics as the book's heroine. Elimelech choose a path of disobedience, fleeing the promised land in a faithless effort to preserve himself. In him, we see a third way in which God's agency works in the historical process. As often as he raises up the righteous for deliverance, so, too, does he accomplish his purposes through the actions of the wicked. Elimelech's disobedience in the face of the famine is what led to Ruth's entrance into the story. Miraculously, not only did Elimelech's misguided decision fail to thwart the divine plan, it actually accomplished it. God frequently works through self-serving, sinful, and even evil individuals to accomplish his purposes in history. In Exodus, we see God's sovereignty graphically on display as he hardens Pharaoh's heart. God gives Pharaoh over to his own depravity in order for the deliverance of his people and to accomplish his own glory. The opening of Isaiah 45 begins with God's message to Cyrus the Great, the pagan king of Persia: "Thus says the Lord to his anointed, to Cyrus, whose right hand I have grasped to subdue nations before him" (Isa 45:1a). Cyrus, a wicked king of a wicked empire, was anointed by God for his divine purpose. Though Cyrus was motivated by his own ambition, it was through him that God brought his people back into the land of promise. When we look over the span of history and see the rise of wicked men, of Stalins, Maos, Hitlers, and others, and when we see the wicked exalted in our own time, we should not fear. The very hand of God that works deliverance through his servants is as much in charge of those who reject him, and his purpose shines as brightly through the wicked as through the righteous.

The Ruth story does not end with the death of the book's characters. Rather, the rest of the historical books of the Old Testament recount the lives of the royal dynasty that began with Ruth. When we trace those lines to the end of the nations of Israel and Judah, we see a final way in which God works in human history. Many of Israel and Judah's kings—most notably Ahab and

Manasseh—were wicked men who led their people away from God. In their fallenness, the nations of Israel and Judah collapsed. Yet as the captives are being led away to Babylon, and the hope of redemption seems lost, God's sovereignty still reigns supreme. We serve a patient, long-suffering God who desires to restore his lost people to fellowship with him. Yet when our hearts become hardened, and we have given ourselves over to sin, the mercy of God is spent, and his judgment shines forth. In these times, God raises up the wicked as a judgment against his people. The evil of rulers such as Ahab and Manasseh reveal God's work of wrath in the historical process. This is something we need to also keep in mind as we observe the rise of tyrants in history. We acknowledge God as sovereign, and rejoice that he is working all for the good of those who love him (Rom 8:28), yet we must also learn to rejoice in his judgment. God's wrath at sin, his zeal for his own holiness, is as much a part of his divine character as his mercy. Too often, we search in vain for deliverance from evil when, in fact, that evil is intended as chastisement. Amidst this gloom, however, there is a picture of hope. God's judgment and his mercy are not mutually exclusive facets of his character. Rather, the temporal judgment of God in this world—as it works itself out through the historical process—is intended as a last-ditch effort to propel us back to the divine. As we witness evil unfold in the history around us, and we acknowledge it as the hand of a wrathful God, history becomes a strong call to repentance and, subsequently, deliverance. The prosperity of evil in history, the rubbish heap beheld by Benjamin's angel, should point us back to the one who controls the storm.

These four examples do not exhaust the mechanisms God deploys in working in human history. They do, however, provide a framework through which we can glimpse the purposes of God in history. We should be cautious, however, about trying to pinpoint the precise divine motivations in specific events in history. For example, it is a dangerous exercise to attempt to ascertain with certainty what God sought to accomplish in the Holocaust. God's ways are infinite and inscrutable, and his purposes are beyond our knowing. We must delight in the sovereignty of God; but we must not make any claim to know the mind of the sovereign.

We can now begin to see why studying the past is so important for the Christian. Simply by acknowledging God's sovereignty, even if we can't see the exact purpose, points us to eternity. Merely asking, "Where is God in the chaos of history?" reveals the existence of God, for "although as time-dwellers we see God's work in tantalizing flashes, the very fact that we can ask about the whole design and long to see it, is evidence that we are not entirely prisoners of our world. In more promising words, it is evidence of not only how but for whom we have been made."[8] Accepting God's sovereignty in human history allows us to frame history as an extension of God's self-revelation through the created order. As the Christian biologist may see the handwork of God in the blooming of a flower, the flight of a hummingbird, or the quiet still of a forest, or a Christian astrophysicist stand in awe at the finger of God on display in the workings of the galaxies, so, too, can Christians come to know God more fully through a study of the past.

THE CHALLENGE OF DIVINE SOVEREIGNTY

For many, the sovereignty of God may seem off-putting. If we submit that God retains absolute control over human affairs, of both the wicked and the righteous, what room is there for human agency? Are we not mere pawns in a divine drama? These are heavy questions that have troubled theologians for centuries, and I in no way wish to suggest that they can be solved in this limited space. Nor do I wish to sweep them under the rug. But our desire for human agency is a product of our own historical epoch, a period in which we elevate self above the group, and ultimately above the divine. When we seek to insert ourselves and our own agency into the historical process, we move away from a Christian theology of history and drift dangerously close to the territory of

---

8. Kidner, *Ecclesiastes*, 79.

postmodernism, seeking to create our own truths and identities apart from the divine reality.

Far from being off-putting, acknowledging that God's sovereignty over the course of history subsumes human agency should comfort us. No Hitler, Stalin, or other sinful man or woman (myself included!) can stand supreme. Only the God of mercy can do that. We can rest assured in the knowledge that the God of the universe is working over and against the forces of humanity, grounded in its own sinfulness, for our redemption. Think of the inconsequential nature of the sparrow. Even this smallest of birds falls under the sovereignty of God: the divine eye beholds and sheds a tear at its passing (Matt 10:29). How much more so for those of us he created in his image! The sovereign nature of our God should be our joy and, as we study the ups and downs of history, our comfort.

This does not entirely negate our responsibility. Recognizing God's sovereignty in history should not lead to complacency on our part. We should never adopt the attitude that God will take care of things and, by so doing, disengage ourselves from being agents of his kingdom in this world. Rather, a theology of history that magnifies God's sovereignty should ground us in the corporeal. Think of the obedience of Ruth, the wisdom of Naomi, and the humble submission of Mary. All of these individuals were guided by God's grace, strengthened by his will, and chosen to be his instruments, yet action was required from all of them. While Christ is king, we are his ambassadors, and we are called to take part in the establishment of his kingdom, with all its glorious ideals, in the here-and-now. We should fight passionately for a just society, leave no despot unchallenged, and strive for peace and equality as a means of glorifying God in the outworking of his kingdom. Yet when these efforts fail and society turns to darkness, while we continue to fight, we can draw comfort from the fact that behind the angel of history's mad tumbling is a grand design striving for the glory of God and the realization of our ultimate hope: an eternity of fellowship with him. We confess that, "'Jesus Christ is the same yesterday and today and forever' (Heb 13:8), but this founds the Christian hope that men may begin to share in his Resurrection now and in the past and future of human history, [not only] in a timeless life after death."[9] So act now! Allow yourself to be used by God as he works in history, even as you acknowledge and delight in his sovereign control.

CONCLUSION

A Christian theology of history that submits Christ as the hermeneutic through which we read the human past and accepts God's sovereignty as a counter to the postmodern axiom of the subjectivity of truth reforms the goal of our study of history. Secular histories focus on the story of man, are beset by chaos and disorder, and, while they may provide inchoate explanatory frameworks for understanding the past, ring hollow in their fruitless striving to establish human agency. A Christian theology of history declares God as the creator, mover, purpose, and logic of history. In the divine drama, God, the director, calls us into the unfolding of the human story as actors and as spectators. We must learn to delight in both of these roles.

A Christian study of the past should lead us to Christ, for "Christ is the focal point of history." With this in mind, we confess that Christ "is also and at the same time over and in control of history. It is his story and contains his meaning. It is our privilege to enter into that history consciously through faith in him."[10] And what a privilege that is! We are called to behold the workings of God as he enters the human drama, not only in redemptive history, but in the whole of history itself. As we look to the past, we catch a glimpse of God, see his character, and rejoice in who he is, what he does, and what he is doing. We do not see the rubbish heap that the blinded angel of history vainly attempts to comprehend, but a mountain of grace as a longsuffering God works out his plan for his glory and for our deliverance. Here, then, is the Christian call to study history: look to the past, and behold our great God!

9. Lewry, *Theology of History*, 10.
10. Lewry, *Theology of History*, 56.

3

Where was God in the Holocaust? The Narrative of History and the Question of Theodicy

"The idols of the nineteenth century have disintegrated, and man is once again without direction and without a convincing goal. The calamities that have befallen our generation have bred disillusionment and cynicism. Some people, however, have started looking for a new anchor for their lives; they are searching for a purpose on earth. In their misery and confusion, men have naturally turned to religion."[1]

"Those who cry out in grief to God, consciously or unconsciously, join in the dying cry of Jesus Christ, 'My God, why have you forsaken me?' Those who recognize this immediately feel that God is not that unfathomable Other in heaven, but is in a very personal sense the human God who cries with them, and the sympathetic Spirit who cries in them and will go on crying for them when they themselves are silenced. It is the comfort of the crucified Christ that he brings the love of God, and the fellowship of the eternal Spirit into the abysses of our suffering and our

---

1. Berkovits, *God, Man, and History*, 3. This comes from a work written shortly after the Holocaust, as intellectuals around the world grappled with the profound questions that arise from such a gross display of human evil.

hells of evil, so that we do not go under in pain but change suffering to life, whether here or there."[2]

"Who is this that darkens counsel by words without knowledge? Dress for action like a man; I will question you, and you make it known to me. Where were you when I laid the foundation of the earth? Tell me, if you have understanding. Who determined its measurements—surely you know! Or who stretched the line upon it?" (Job 38:2–5)

IN HIS GROUNDBREAKING MONOGRAPH on the Holocaust, Christopher Browning recalls the testimony of a metalworker from Bremerhaven, Germany who took part in the atrocities. The middle-aged man was a member of Reserve Battalion 101, which had been called to Poland to participate in the Final Solution— Hitler's systematic plan for the elimination of Jews in his newly established empire. In the early stages of the Holocaust, Jews were led from the ghettos in which they lived to the forest to be shot, a process that radically transformed the lives of those participating in the killings. Their postwar testimonies offer a glimpse into the evil that was one of the darkest chapters of the twentieth century and reflect the depravity of which human beings are capable. The Bremerhaven laborer's account is particularly troubling: "I made the effort, and it was possible for me, to shoot only children. It so happened that the mothers led the children by the hand. My neighbor then shot the mother and I shot the child that belonged to her, because I reasoned with myself that, after all, without its mother, the child could not live any longer. It was supposed to be, so to speak, soothing to my conscience to release children unable to live without their mothers."[3] Browning adds that "the full weight of this statement, and the significance of the word choice of the former policeman, cannot be fully appreciated unless one knows that the German world for 'release' (erlösen) also means to 'redeem' or 'save' when used in a religious sense. The one who 'releases' is

2. Moltmann, *History*, 29–30.
3. Browning, *Ordinary Men*, 73.

the *Erlöser*—the Savior or redeemer!"[4] Words cannot express the depravity of the twisted logic through which one positions oneself in a messianic role while willfully murdering a child after witnessing the killing of the child's mother.

As Christians looking to the past, seeking to glimpse the divine, what are we to make of accounts like this? In the previous chapter, we asserted that not only is God sovereign over all of history but he is also fundamentally good and works all of human history together for his plan. But this seems to contradict the testimony given above. If God is good, and he directs the course of history, how can events like the Holocaust happen? A reasonable person may be able to ascent to the fact that a good God can allow a measure of bad in the world. We would never question God's goodness after stubbing our toes or crashing our bicycles. Perhaps we can even accept the passing away of elderly relatives. But horrors on the level of the Holocaust have led many to question the existence of God, his good nature, or his sovereignty. Theologians have debated long before the Final Solution about the tension between God's goodness and sovereignty, and certainly these issues cannot be resolved in the space of this chapter. Yet if we are to develop and apply a Christian theology of history, we must engage in this debate. We will not reach a tidy answer by the time of our conclusion. Instead, this chapter argues that history provides a narrative medium through which we can engage the question of theodicy, and thereby points us toward an understanding of a good God who allows suffering in his world.

NARRATIVE AND THE QUESTION OF THEODICY

At this point, we have transitioned from a postmodern view of history to a Christian one. We established the absolute sovereignty of God as the axiom for developing a Christian theology of history. Accepting divine authorship over the historical process, however, leads to a host of existential dilemmas, the chief of which is the

---

4. Browning, *Ordinary Men*, 73.

question of theodicy. If God is the all-powerful director of the human story, and if we serve a God who is fundamentally good, why is history marred with tragedy?

The story of the human past, contrary to the oft-preached teleological, triumphalist narratives of history (an approach that dominates common perceptions of American history), is an endless string of human suffering, case study after case study of the wicked inclinations of the hearts of men and women unfettered by morality. As we look to the past and see such unspeakable horror (punctuated, occasionally, with a breath of nobility, the emergence of the rare case of a person acting in, rather than against, the image of God), the indomitable question of theodicy arises. Surely a God of mercy, a God of love, a God eager to spend his wrath on himself rather than his fallen creation, and a God who is sovereign over kings, empires, and every minutia of the human experience, could have spared a moment to restrain the worst of human evil and provide repose from the gravest of vice?

How is it possible to provide an answer to such a probing question? And how does the question of theodicy interact with a Christian theology of history? In her masterful work on the theodicy debate, philosopher Eleonore Stump posits that "narrative makes a contribution to philosophical reflection that cannot be gotten as well, or at all, without the narrative."[5] Stump deftly employs several accounts from scripture, including the book of Job and the story of Lazarus's death, to demonstrate how narrative approaches to the question of theodicy mediate the question better than strictly abstract philosophical methodologies. Stump's approach can inform a Christian study of the past. History, littered as it is by stories of gross human suffering, provides a narrative medium through which to engage the question of theodicy. It is impossible for humanity in its finite, fallen nature to lay hold of God's sovereignty in our suffering. In a sense, then, we must accept the apparent tension between God's sovereignty and goodness without full understanding. The historical narrative, however, provides a means through which we can catch a glimpse of the mind,

5. Stump, *Wandering in Darkness*, xviii.

and, more importantly, the heart, of the divine. History provides us the opportunity to, like Job, question God in faith, a safe arena in which we can air our doubts. In this probing, history can lead us to hope. This hope is not anchored in the inevitable progress of history, a thought at which Benjamin's angel scoffs, but rather finds its fullness in the striving of the outworking of the kingdom of God inaugurated in Christ as it marches toward its full culmination at the close of time.

Philosophizing alone will never produce a satisfactory answer to the question of theodicy. Narrative is required to put flesh on the skeleton of the debate. We must nuance the relationship between God's goodness and his sovereignty within the context of actual human experience. History, then, becomes a space in which we can interrogate theodicy in concrete terms. Thus, we can study the past—and, in particular, events like the Holocaust—not only as an academic exercise to satisfy our curiosity. As Christians who are called to engage with history, our study of the past is as much a theological exercise as an intellectual one. The past should constantly point us back to the Lord of history, to cause us to ask the profound questions that, if left unanswered, draw us to the same hopelessness as Benjamin's angel. Like the prophet Habakkuk, we may question God's goodness in our collective suffering, asking: "O Lord, how long shall I cry for help, and you will not hear? Or cry to you 'Violence!' and you will not save?" (Hab 1:2). The past provides a revelatory medium through which God provides an inchoate answer to this question and leads us to the same plea as the prophet: "O Lord, I have heard the report of you, and your work, O Lord, do I fear. In the midst of the years revive it; in the midst of the years make it known; in wrath, remember mercy" (Hab 3:2).

APPROACHES TO THE QUESTION OF THEODICY

Before we can begin to see how studying the Holocaust can grow our faith, we must first establish how our faith impacts our view of the Holocaust. Applying the theology of history developed in the previous chapter, I must make several bold—perhaps even controversial—claims. First, I assert that if God is sovereign over all history, then God was sovereign over the Holocaust. This is not to say, as some have done in the past, that God *caused* the Holocaust. Such a statement would be inappropriate, offensive, and would pervert a true understanding of God's sovereignty. God is not the origin of evil but still retains sovereignty and agency within the bounds of his fallen creation. Evil is a product of the devil and entered into the human story through Adam's fall. Nevertheless, in his grace, God reigns over *and* through the wicked.

The second claim builds on the first and asserts that not only did God retain sovereignty over the Holocaust but, like all of his work in history, he had *purposeful* agency as well. That is, the Holocaust was not a meaningless tragedy but rather folds into the divine plan. This is an extraordinarily uncomfortable thought and an especially controversial position. In the decades since the Holocaust, numerous antisemitic theologians have asserted possible divine motivations for the Holocaust that center on God's punishment of the Jews, usually for their supposed guilt incurred by crucifying Christ. This is not the claim I am making here, and such a claim should be vehemently rejected and opposed. Yet we must, uncomfortable as it is, assert that God not only acts but also has purpose, and this applies to even the darkest episode of history.

The final claim I wish to make is that God's goodness is not compromised by his sovereignty. God's goodness, like his sovereignty, is intrinsic to his nature. What is more, God's goodness is displayed through his sovereignty. His purposeful intervention in our world flows from his mercy, not against it. To make sense of the apparent tension of this third claim with the first two, it is helpful to look at the historical event of the crucifixion. At the very hour that every host of evil rejoiced, when history became so dark that the very sun refused to shine, God retained sovereignty. If we are willing and able to ascent to God's sovereignty over the death of his own son, we must be willing to see it at work during other times when it appears as if Satan has been given free reign. Again, this is not to suggest that God creates evil. Rather, an omnipotent God is able to restrict his sovereignty to work within the parameters of his own fallen creation. Evil in the world derives from our own sinfulness. God does not create sin—that is a product of our own nature, which is less than divine—but drafts the drama of history within a world that is marred by sin in order to work out his purpose of destroying sin. But this still leaves us in a difficult place. If God's sovereignty springs forth from his goodness (and vice versa), why is there still suffering, especially the scale of misery of the Holocaust?

Theologians have posited a number of different frameworks that seek to make sense of this difficulty. A commonly held position maintains that, while God permits evil in this world, he does not condone it. At first glance, this seems to provide a satisfactory answer. It accounts for the presence of evil in the world while forbidding it divine sanction. However, this is a half-hearted view of God's sovereignty. It sanctions God's authority to prevent an event like the Holocaust, but denies divine culpability—and, thus, sovereignty—without attempting to explain God's apparent unwillingness to prevent suffering. To be any sort of meaningful deity at all, God must do more than simply permit or deny evil: both good *and* evil must somehow be subsumed under his agency and redound to his glory.

This points us to a lesson about the interplay between God's sovereignty and goodness. Too often asserting these seemingly contradictory facets of the divine character in events like the Holocaust causes discomfort for us because we position human beings at the center of history. If history were merely a story of humanity, the Holocaust may call into question God's goodness. But just as Ruth was not the main character of the book bearing her name, neither is man the main character of history. History is the story of the godhead, a masterful disclosure of the divine nature in the human drama. While our Father certainly cares for us, and is consumed with love for us, we remain secondary characters that call attention to a greater story and glory.

A second framework offered by theologians seeking to find meaning in episodes like the Holocaust is that suffering is redemptive in nature. This position claims that our sufferings in the progress of human life are miniature versions of the cross, the ultimate event of redemptive suffering. Suffering, though brought about by evil, is not intended for evil but rather for good. This answer differs from the previous in that it maintains God's sovereignty over the historical process while seeking purpose behind events like the Holocaust. But is this really a satisfactory answer? When we see the horrors of Auschwitz, the killing fields of Cambodia, the bodies of black men and women hanging from trees in America, does it do justice to the victims to declare that these were merely God's way of drawing us closer to him, examples of redemptive suffering? Must God really be so cruel in the outworking of his plan? Certainly, much suffering is redemptive in nature, and God often wills the suffering of his people to draw them closer to him (Deut 8:5; Isa 48:10–11). As a parent, I have found that the countless sleepless nights and myriad of other struggles that accompany raising children has brought me closer to God. Yet my sufferings are hopelessly trite in comparison with those affected by events like the Holocaust.

This is where history as a narrative medium becomes important. History is complex, nuanced, and abhors simplistic explanations. Historical narrative lays itself at our feet, in all of its messiness, without demanding a conclusive answer. When the Christian looks to the past and sees the Holocaust and other tragic events, he or she can embrace the complexity of the human situation. We need to caution ourselves against providing meme-friendly explanations to questions as deep as "Where was God in the Holocaust?" We must address suffering in all its dimensions, with all its complexities, and, in so doing, acknowledge the grandeur and scope of the divine design, the far reaches of the fingers of God within the historical process.

Does this mean that posing the question is a fruitless endeavor? Far from it! Job spent a good portion of the book that bears his name questioning both God's sovereignty and his goodness. By the end of the book, God neither condemns Job's doubts nor provides an answer to reconcile the apparently contradictory facts of the divine character. We, like Job, are permitted to put God on trial. The study of history provides an occasion in which to pose these questions and work toward an inchoate response. Studying the past, then, impacts our faith by allowing us to air our doubts and, in the process, to draw nearer to the divine.

THE THEOLOGY OF HISTORY AND THE QUESTION OF SUFFERING

Beyond providing a medium in which to mediate the tension between God's goodness and his sovereignty, a historical narrative approach to the question of theodicy elevates the experiences of those who have suffered. Theological approaches to the question of theodicy tend to focus on philosophical questions about the nature of God and provide answers focused on reconciling the different facets of the divine character. But suffering is not only philosophical in nature. Rather, suffering touches real lives, and any approach to the question of theodicy must address the stories of those impacted by events like the Holocaust.

Theologies of suffering not firmly anchored in the historical experience run the risk of being used as a means of trapping individuals in their suffering. Too often, Christians have taught the oppressed to join their sufferings to Christ's sacrifice in order to nullify resistance. In the Antebellum south, slave masters taught their slaves that to be good Christians, they had to willfully submit to their enslavement. But a true Christian theology of suffering, informed by the historical experience, demands more than resigned suffering out of a misguided sense of Christian duty. Rather, history reveals that the question of theodicy must be met with a cry for justice for the oppressed, for those who suffer grave injustices. A historical narrative approach to the question of theodicy counters the claim that a Christian view of suffering that preserves the sovereignty and goodness of God enables the perpetuation of human suffering. Firstly, it draws attention to the ultimate event of human history—the incarnation—wherein the God who seems far off draws near and enters into our suffering. Secondly, a historical-narrative approach to the question of theodicy gives voice to the suffering, allowing them to draft their own story vis-à-vis their oppressors, and provides a channel for redress.

Christian approaches to the question of theodicy have often emphasized Christ's suffering as an answer to the cries of those who suffer. But rather than asserting that Christ suffered and therefore we, too, must suffer, or maintaining that our sufferings redemptively join with Christ's sufferings, we need to ask, "Does this suffering of Christ in solidarity with the victims of the history of human violence have any significance for the victims?"[6] Moltmann answers that, "If [Christ] were just one more victim, then his suffering would have no particular significance. But if God himself is *in Christ* (2 Cor 5:19), then Christ brings eternal communion with God and God's life-giving righteousness through his passion into the passion story of this world and identifies God with the victims of violence. Conversely, we also have here the identification of the victims with God, so that they are put under divine protection, and though lacking human rights, have rights with God."[7] Rather than conceptualizing the sufferings of Christ and human suffering as existing on parallel planes, we need to read the incarnation as being indicative of God's entrance *into* our suffering. This submits more than the fact that, through Christ, God knows what it is like to suffer. Rather, the outgrowth of the kingdom of God as inaugurated at the incarnation is the beginning of the end of human suffering. Not only does Christ meet us in our suffering, he refuses to leave us there. He descended to the very depths of hell to claim his own, and works from then through the present to destroy evil in this world. We must remember that the king of history wears a crown of thorns.

History reclaims the narrative of the suffering, giving power and witness to the voices of those who suffer. A historical narrative approach to history gives weight to the experiences of victims and provides an avenue of justice and redress. In Stump's reading of Lazarus's death, she envisions Christ entering into the grief of Lazarus's sisters, Mary and Martha. Important as this christological

6. Moltmann, *History*, 48.

7. Moltmann, *History*, 48.

perspective is, the narrative also elevates the voice of these women, giving them the power to lay their suffering at Jesus' feet and cry for justice. In a similar manner, historical narrative provides a vehicle through which those who have experienced suffering can begin the process of justice. We see examples of this in the testimonies of those imprisoned at Auschwitz and other internment camps, in South Africa's post-apartheid Truth and Reconciliation Committees, and indeed wherever victims of injustice force their accounts into the historical record, challenging the narrative of the oppressor and enabling a renewed future in which justice is achieved.

Engaging the question of theodicy vis-à-vis those who suffer in the course of human history thus reveals another reason Christians should be concerned with the past. But it also provides us with a framework for how we should engage history. If Christian historical inquiry necessitates elevating the experience of those who suffer, then, as Christians, we should privilege the stories of the marginalized as we engage the past. Historical inquiry over much of the last century has too often been a triumphalist narrative of the west. History is taught as being white, male, heterosexual, Christian, and cis-gender. History has been packaged as the story of privilege. But there has been a marvelous awakening in the historical discipline that is only now beginning to give life to the experiences of those who existed outside of the traditional spheres of power in the western world. We have covered some of the reasons for this awakening when we talked about postmodernism. Here, we need to submit to the need for a decidedly Christian focus on studying the silenced, those whose lives were marked by suffering, who stood outside of the realms of power within history, those trampled on by Benjamin's angel, for these are precisely those with whom Christ, the Lord and focus of history, most identifies. A Christian approach to the question of suffering should lead us to focus on these histories, and focusing on the histories of those rejected by society should throw us straight into the person of Christ.

WHERE WAS GOD IN THE HOLOCAUST?

Having submitted that history provides a narrative medium through which we can engage the question of theodicy, and having seen how historical inquiry enhances our understanding of theology of suffering, we have yet to answer the question, "Where was God in the Holocaust?" and we may not be able to reach a consensus, for events as marked by horror as the Holocaust defy rational explanation. Yet as we look to the narrative of history to engage the question of theodicy, we discover some basic principles about the tension between God's sovereignty and goodness as seen in the Holocaust and other graphic episodes in human history. Firstly, we learn that God's sovereignty is a mystery to delight in, and we must avoid over guessing at what his hand is doing. The finite human mind will never be able to fully grasp the purposes behind God's providence, yet we are called to rejoice in it anyway. Think back to the story of Ruth and the suffering therein. Israel goes through a grave famine, and Naomi and Elimelech must leave the promised land. Elimelech and his sons die. Neither Ruth nor Naomi could see God's purpose. Eventually, Ruth may perhaps have been able to perceive that through this suffering she is able to come to an encounter with the God of Israel. Sometimes we can catch glimpses of God's purpose in our suffering. Yet what Ruth could never have imagined was that this lifetime of suffering she shared with Naomi prepared the way for the birth of the savior of mankind, the one who came to put an end to Ruth's suffering. The divine purpose was located generations in the future, a deliverance that could not be seen in the suffering of the moment. While we can sometimes see part of God's purposes, we can never imagine the bigger picture for his glory that he has behind these episodes.

Secondly, a historical narrative approach to the question of theodicy vis-à-vis the Holocaust reveals that suffering is transformational. The horrors of the Holocaust ushered in a new episteme in world history. Gone were the legacies of the old order that gave rise to both world wars. In their place came the newly minted United Nations, the rise of the concept of human rights, and an era of

mass decolonization. Surely all was not perfect. The end of World
War II inaugurated a new phase in the Cold War as the temporary
alliance between the United States and the Soviet Union collapsed.
The ushering in of the nuclear age left the world on the brink of destruction, and the bipolar division of power led to devastating conflicts from Korea to Vietnam to the Congo. The prosperity of the
post-war years brought unprecedented destruction to the natural
world, creating an environmental headache from which we may
never recover. But for all the bad, we should be encouraged by the
world that emerged following the Holocaust, for we can learn that
evil lasts for but a season. God has securely promised that he will
not fully give his creation over to evil again for their own destruction (Gen 8:21), and this means that he necessarily restrains evil to
have a finite impact. What is more, from the darkness often comes
light. As the apostles witnessed their master's crucifixion, one
can imagine that they lost any semblance of hope. Evil seemed to
win with every anguished cry that escaped their beloved teacher's
mouth. As his head fell in death, they must have imagined that all
hope was over. Yet as Ruth could never have anticipated the coming glory in her own suffering, a glory that lay generations away,
neither, too, could the disciples grasp what was to come next. We
must keep this in mind as we study the Holocaust and other such
events: evil will not last forever, and light often follows darkness,
even if the light is shadowed by new clouds.

CONCLUSION

There is much more that Christians can learn from studying the
Holocaust through the lens of God's sovereignty. In the next chapter, we will interrogate what we can learn from the past, and in so
doing will use the Holocaust as a case study for seeing what history
can teach us. For the moment, we must pause and reflect on what
we have grasped to this point.

The central argument of this book is that Christians have
much to gain from studying the past. Our discussion of the narrative of history and the question of theodicy reveals that Christian

engagement with the past provides a vehicle through which we can transform our faith from idea to praxis. The past provides a rich tapestry of stories that reveal the mysteries of God's interaction with his fallen creation. Even as we encounter the worst of humanity in the past, we can still see God at work. This teaches us two things. Firstly, as we go through our own difficulties, the loss of a spouse or job, a crushing diagnosis, or any of the other trials that assail us in our individual lives, or when we look at our nation and see rampant and rising racism, economic crisis, and environmental disaster, we should work toward a solution, for sure, but we may rest confident that the sovereign hand of God is still at work, and that evil lasts only for a moment. Secondly, as we behold the sovereign hand of God in evil, we can ponder the mystery that is our God. Who is a God like him (Mic 7:18–19)? Our eyes may fail to perceive him and we may join Benjamin's angel in despair at the chaos that we mistakenly call progress, yet we may still rest confident in the God of history, the God who entered human history. This is the same God who calmed and who will calm the storm that assails the angel of history as he draws the human story to its climax, restoring his fallen creation to himself. All this is on display if we look to the past with eyes of faith.

In the end, as we pose the question as to where God was in the Holocaust, we can draw strength from the story of Job in the Bible. God's response to Job's questioning at the end of the book contains some of the most powerful words in scripture, yet it is too often overlooked. As Job in faith questioned God's goodness, God turned to him and took him on a sweeping tour of the created order. Was Job present at creation? Was Job there when the mountain goat gave birth? Has Job seen heavenly storehouses laden with snow? God asserts his sovereignty as the answer to Job's suffering. Proffering God's sovereignty as the answer to the theodicy debate does not give us the "why" of the Holocaust that we so earnestly seek. Yet as we embrace divine sovereignty as we plough through these theological difficulties, we find ourselves encountering the "who" of history. This is precisely the benefit to a historical narrative approach to theodicy. We may fail to discern a clear answer to our original question, but we walk away having met face-to-face with the one who holds that answer.

4

Heroes and Villains:
What is the Lesson of History?

"Progress, far from consisting in change, depends on retentiveness. When change is absolute there remains no being to improve and no direction is set for possible improvement: and when experience is not retained, as among savages, infancy is perpetual. Those who cannot remember the past are condemned to repeat it."[1]

"Should we be confident, now that a Holocaust is behind us, that a recognizable future awaits? We share a world with the forgotten perpetrators as well as with the memorialized victims. The world is now changing, reviving fears that were familiar in Hitler's time, and to which Hitler responded. The history of the Holocaust is not over. Its precedent is eternal, and its lessons have not yet been learned."[2]

"The godly has perished from the earth, and there is no one upright among mankind; they all lie in wait for blood, and each hunts the other with a net. Their hands are on what is evil, to do it well; the prince and the judge ask for a bribe, and the great man utters the evil desire of his

1. Santayana, *Life of Reason*, 284.
2. Snyder, *Black Earth*, xii.

soul; thus they weave it together." (Mic 7:2–4)

I BEGIN EVERY SEMESTER with my world history students by engaging them in a discussion to sort out what history is all about. Chiefly, I am interested in leading my students, most of whom are forced to take the class as part of a general education program, into an understanding that history *can* and *should* be a meaningful part of their daily lives. Thus, I pose the question, "Why do you think you should study history?" (One must be careful to not ask "Why are you here?" for the inevitable answer to that question is a snide "I had to take this class.")

Invariably, multiple students will answer with different versions of the (in)famous George Santayana quote: "Those who cannot remember the past are condemned to repeat it." I am convinced that most of my students, if any, neither know the origins of the quote nor care to know that, in its original context, it included a racist remark about non-European societies (see above). My students—and many others, I suspect—believe that the true meaning behind studying history is to figure out all of the stupid, unproductive things that human beings have done, and then, subsequently, to not do those things. This thinking is misdirected. History does not provide a meta-answer to the human condition. Rather, the lesson of history points us toward the one who alone can provide that answer as it opens the eyes of our hearts to our own depravity.

The thesis of this book is that studying the past is a profitable endeavor for Christians. In the past chapter, we examined the ways in which the historical narrative can help navigate the question of theodicy, using the Holocaust as an example. History, then, is meaningful for Christians because it provides a vehicle through which we can engage profound questions of our faith. Throughout our discussion, we danced around a question that will become the subject of this chapter: what can we learn from studying the past? Specifically, is there some grand lesson, such as the one envisioned by Santayana and my students, which Christians ought to derive from the historical narrative? For the sake of familiarity, we will once again use the Holocaust as a case study through which to engage this question.

REPEATING THE ERRORS OF THE PAST

To devise an answer to the question "What is the lesson of history?" it is helpful to begin with a specific event, the Holocaust, and then trace its lessons. Once we unpack the lessons specific to this discrete event, we can abstract those lessons and construct an answer to the original query. And since I have already put forth the most common sentiment on what the lesson of the past is, namely that we can learn from it and not repeat it, we shall begin by scrutinizing that sentiment.

Is it important to study the Holocaust lest we repeat it? This refrain certainly has dominated popular histories of the Holocaust study and is present in the official memory of the event. Politicians, writers, academics, and clergy clamor that from the ashes of the Holocaust must emerge a strong sense of "Never again!" that as we see the evils that marked this darkest episode of history, we must commit ourselves to prevent its repeat. Indeed, whenever there is a new episode of mass killing—in Cambodia, in Palestine, in Bosnia, in Kosovo—world leaders invoke the Holocaust and call on humanity to not repeat its destruction.

The refrain of "Never Again!" is at best a weak answer to the question of what can be learned from the Holocaust and does a profound disservice to those whose lives were lost in this horrific event. Certainly we don't want a repeat of this mass killing, but how are we to accomplish that? I do not need history to teach me that killing six million Jews is objectively wrong. In fact, as I often remonstrate to my students, if a person does not find such an action abhorrent *before* studying the Holocaust, we have reason to seriously question that person! Further, many of the twentieth-centuries worst killers—including Stalin, Mao, and Pol Pot—were well aware of the history of the Holocaust, and yet still went on to commit heinous crimes against humanity. Indeed, Hitler himself was keenly aware of the history of mass violence that preceded him, yet still committed his unspeakable crimes. Speaking of his plans to invade Poland and eastern Russia as part of his quest for *lebensraum* (living space, i.e., an expanded Germany), the execution of which laid the foundations for the Final Solution and the murder of six million Jews, Hitler turned to the history of the Armenian genocide of 1915:

> I have issued the command—and I'll have anybody who utters but one word of criticism executed by a firing squad—that our war aim does not consist in reaching certain lines, but in the physical destruction of the enemy. Accordingly, I have placed my death head formations in readiness—for the present only in the east—with orders to them to send to death mercilessly and without compassion, men, women, and children of Polish derivation and language. Only thus shall we gain the living space which we need. Who, after all, speaks today of the annihilation of the Armenians?[3]

Knowledge of past atrocities not only failed to turn Hitler from committing greater crimes; rather, knowledge of the past is what spurred him on. Shining light on the past, then, provides no guarantee that we will not repeat many of its follies.

Santayana's sentiment sounds appealing, but it doesn't hold ground when met with real examples from history. Those who study history *may* commit many of the same crimes that they have read about, and history fails to provide us with an objective moral lesson that we could not have otherwise described. As much as we want to display the deep wound on humanity that was the Holocaust, hoping that those who bear witness to its depravity would vow "never again," the wickedness of human nature (Gen 6:5) means that the hearts of many who study the Holocaust may remain hard and, in spite of what they have seen through the looking glass of the past, may engage in mass violence. History without the gospel cannot restrain evil.

If history is not required to prevent the orchestrators of mass violence from committing the same obvious evils from the past, is

---

3. Lockner, *What about Germany*, 1–4.

it not possible for society as a whole to learn from the pattern of the past that led to such evils? Can we not look to the history of the Holocaust, study the rise of Hitler, see the degradation of an entire society, and then look for those conditions in our own time that we may turn back before driving off the cliff? British novelist and short story writer L. P. Hartley quipped that "the past is a foreign country; they do things differently there."[4] By this he means that the past is an unrecognizable landscape, disconnected linguistically, culturally, and politically from the present. A contemporary American transported back in time to turn-of-the-century America would find herself as disoriented as if she had been whisked away to a foreign country in which she knows neither the language nor the culture. The past is not cyclical; history does not repeat itself.

There is a very real danger in our tendency to read the past into the present. Firstly, we often fall into the trap of making false associations. This can be seen in the frequency within American political discourse that people invoke the label of fascism, a specific historical and political movement that bears only a passing resemblance to any contemporary grabs at power within American society, yet which nevertheless is often deployed as if it were the perfect comparison. More importantly, looking to the past to teach us about our present conditions distracts us from the evils unique to our own epoch. In antebellum America, a majority of society considered slavery to be a normal institution. They failed to see evil within their own time. In a similar manner, when we focus on trying to fit the present into the schematics of the past, we miss those evils peculiar to our time.

The conditions that led to the rise of Hitler and the eventual slaughter of six million Jews as part of his rule are unrepeatable: they were historically conditioned in circumstances drastically different than our own. This is not to say that we are free from the risk of the rise of movements resulting in the deaths of thousands or millions in our own time. Indeed, we have seen violence on a grand scale time and again since the Holocaust. We need to regard

4. Hartley, *Go-Between*, 1.

each discrete episode within its own historical framework to understand the unique conditions that brought it about. We must interrogate the circumstances of our own time and challenge the evils around us that go unchecked.

What does this have to tell us more generally about the lesson of history? We need to recognize that, contrary to popular perceptions, history is *not* cyclical and does not repeat itself. Each new epoch, each new event, each new horror that emerges on the stage of the human drama, is unique, a product of its own time, and conditioned by its own reality. In one sense, then, the preacher in the book of Ecclesiastes is wrong: there always *is* something new under the sun (Eccl 1:9). We are wise to be extraordinarily judicious when attempting to use events from the past to inform contemporary discussions.

HEROES AND VILLAINS: SEEING OURSELVES IN THE PAST

As often as we try to read the past through the lens of the present, we also attempt to project ourselves into the past. One of the chief ways in which individuals engage history is to imagine themselves as participants in the historical drama. To a point, this can be a profitable endeavor, though seeing too much of the present in the past, or vice versa, can be dangerous. There are, however, merits to this approach. History is the grand narrative of humanity, and, as with any tale, it only becomes truly great when the reader feels what is on the page, that is, sees it as if it is happening to herself. This is one reason that historical fiction novels and historically-based films are so successful: the past has the power to speak to us, to move us, when we personally enter into the narratives of those who went before us.

The process by which we imagine ourselves as characters in the past is helpful for understanding what the lesson of history is. Reflecting on what stories draw our attention, what portions of the catalogue of the human experience appeal to us, the stories into which we are willing to insert ourselves, and the characters we identify with, reflects greatly on our self-beliefs in the present. We tend to cast ourselves in the role of the heroes of the past, while denying our capacity to be the villain. But if history has one thing to teach us, if there is any value in studying the past, it is not a lesson in morality, nor is it a chance to learn from the successes and failures of past generations and even civilizations. Rather, history becomes our instructor precisely when it becomes our mirror, that is, when we look to the brokenness of the past, the chapters of the human story in which the triumph of evil clouds out all light, and we begin to see ourselves. History is the great looking-glass through which we can behold our own depravity, a reflecting pool shinning back the cobwebs and dust within our souls that we often ignore and willfully choose to not see.

To illustrate this, we will need to dive into the historiography (the study of the study of history) of the Holocaust and connect this to popular perceptions of the Final Solution in order to begin to understand truly what the event has to teach us. Over the past two and a half decades, two schools of thought have emerged in Holocaust studies concerning the nature of those Germans who participated in the Final Solution. The first was articulated in Christopher Browning's afore mentioned seminal work, *Ordinary Men: Reserve Police Battalion 101 and the Final Solution in Poland*. The 1993 monograph caused a seismic debate in Holocaust studies. It centered on perpetrators, rather than victims, and the motives that caused or, at the very least, enabled them to willfully participate in mass killing. Browning argues that while there were a number of preconditions that *enabled* the Holocaust, including antisemitism, a weakened economy following the First World War, and a renewed German nationalism, none of these factors alone could explain popular participation in killing. Indeed, similar forces were at work throughout much of the western world at the time, yet no other society chose the same path as Germany. Rather, Browning submits that the human machinery of the Holocaust, those men who gathered Jews from the ghettoes of Poland to be transported to death camps, the soldiers who began the Final Solution by shooting Jews in the countryside after they had been removed from the city, and those who drove the Jews to their deaths, were ordinary men. There was nothing in their background prior to World War II that would indicate their potential for mass murder. A series of factors, including wartime conditioning, peer pressure, careerism, and a sense of comradery, allowed these men to slowly develop into hardened killers. Browning describes the process as gradual, with many men visibly ill and unable to proceed after the first round of killings in which they participated. Officers found that they had to slowly introduce men to the process of killing innocent civilians, lest they refuse to con- -tinue or succumb to psychological breakdown.

Browning's work was met with a fiery rebuttal in Daniel Jonah Goldhagen's *Hitler's Willing Executioners*, which was published four years after *Ordinary Men*.[5] Goldhagen revived what had been, in generations past, the consensus view surrounding the motivation of perpetrators. Goldhagen maintains, contrary to Browning, that these were not ordinary men with no predisposition to engage in mass violence. Rather, he emphasizes the role that antisemitism played in the Holocaust, finding it to be one of the prime motivations for participation.

What does this have to teach us about the lesson of history? As we read ourselves into the past, we see ourselves in the world that Goldhagen has created. If the Holocaust was caused only by antisemitism, then we can acquit ourselves of any guilt by establishing that we are not antisemitic. This was an evil of which we are not capable. But if Browning's outlook is correct, if the Holocaust was carried out by men and women just like us, then we, too, are capable of the same great evil. Browning has landed at this same conclusion, stating at the outset of his book that "the policemen in the battalion who carried out the massacres and deportations, like the much smaller number who refused or evaded, were human beings. I must recognize that in the same situation, I could have been either a killer or an evader—both were humans."[6] Later, he fleshes out how this provides a lesson to us:

5. See Goldhagen, *Hitler's Willing Executioner*.
6. Browning, *Ordinary Men*, xx.

At the same time, however, the collective behavior of Reserve Police Battalion 101 has deeply disturbing implications. There are many societies afflicted by traditions of racism and caught in the siege mentality of war or threat of war. Everywhere society conditions people to respect and defer to authority, and indeed could scarcely function otherwise. Everywhere people seek career advancement. In every modern society, the complexity of life and the resulting bureaucratization and specialization attenuate the sense of personal responsibility of those implementing official policy. Within virtually every social collective, the peer group exerts tremendous pressures on behavior and sets moral norms. If the men of Reserve Police Battalion 101 could become killers under such circumstances, what group of men cannot?[7]

Given the right circumstance, each and every one of us has the capacity to commit the same acts as the men of Reserve Battalion 101.

It is easy when studying the history of the Holocaust to imagine that, were we alive at the time, we would have been one of the individuals saving Jews, not the person pulling the trigger. Prominent Holocaust historian Timothy Snyder has captured this sentiment and is worth quoting at length, ultimately concluding that it is faulty:

> The idea of rescue seems close to us; the ideology of murder seems distant. Ecological panic, state destruction, colonial racism, and global antisemitism might seem exotic. Most people in Europe and North America live in functional states, taking for granted the basic elements of sovereignty that preserved the lives of Jews and others during the war: foreign policy, citizenship, and bureaucracy. After two generations, the Green Revolution has removed the fear of hunger from the emotions of electorates and the vocabulary of politicians. The open expression of antisemitic ideas is a taboo in much of the West, if perhaps a receding one. Separated from National Socialism by time and luck, we find it easy to dismiss

7. Browning, *Ordinary Men*, 189.

> Nazi ideas without contemplating how they functioned.
> Our forgetfulness convinces us that we are different from
> Nazis by shrouding the ways that we are the same.[8]

The truth is that those who chose to resist the horrors of the Final Solution were few and far between. Neighbors turned in neighbors, the clergy refused sanctuary to those slated to die, and friends turned on friends. Most disturbing, neither the Protestant nor Catholic church mounted a serious challenge to the Holocaust (Catholics did do marginally more to protest, however), and Christians of all denominations joined in the killing without so much as a verbal objection.

What is the lesson of this specific event in history? What does the history of the Holocaust have to teach us? Can we learn anything from this history? Absolutely! But it is not necessarily a lesson about others, as we often frame it. As Christians, approaching the past—especially a past as dark as the Holocaust—we must learn to examine ourselves. Here we see the central lesson of history for the believer: the wickedness manifested in my own heart as a descendent of Adam could have, indeed, most likely would have, led me to participate in the horrors of events like the Holocaust had God deigned that I be born in a different time and space. History teaches us neither the evils of others nor how to stop evil in this world, but forces us to confront the depravity inherent to us all.

THE LESSON OF HISTORY FOR THE BELIEVER

What principles, then, does this give us for the broader lesson of history? How does a study of the past enrich our faith? As we highlighted in our discussion about the specific lessons of the Holocaust, we first need to begin to position ourselves within the historical narrative not as the heroes, which our prideful nature inclines us toward but rather as the villains. History is the tutor that reveals to us our own sinfulness. But could we not be aware of our

---

8. Snyder, *Black Earth*, 323.

depravity apart from studying the past? Surely we can. There are three ways, however, in which a specifically historical awareness of human depravity can shape and inform our faith.

Firstly, a historically informed awareness of our depravity can help us recover a sense of humility from the past. Twenty-first century American Christians often see themselves as the savior of the world. We (rightly) champion a whole host of social causes with the belief that we are creating a world in the image of God's kingdom. We go on missions trips, fight poverty, and work to end human trafficking all in an attempt to place ourselves on the right side of history. We are correct to do these things, all of which are worthy causes, yet when we explore the lives of our mothers and fathers in the faith (a task we will do in greater detail in the next chapter), we find that many of their efforts were misguided. Missionaries who brought the gospel to Africa at the turn of the twentieth century, an overwhelmingly good objective, often contributed to the spread of the abuses of imperialism on the continent. Christian abolitionists in antebellum America often championed the end of legal slavery yet legitimized and reified racism through their efforts. Beyond these good intentions gone bad, Christians have also directly contributed to many of the greatest ills in human history, including openly supporting and participating in slavery and the Holocaust. The agents and ambassadors of Christ's kingdom too often have aided and strengthened the work of the enemy.

This could lead us to a sense of despair, to a frightened vision of our own depravity. Are all our efforts worthless? Are we destined to fail in our temporal quest for justice? This should not lead us to disengage from kingdom work in the time in which we live. Rather, we must cultivate from our study of history a proper sense of humility regarding our efforts and our capacity for both good and evil. We thereby rejoice in the sovereignty of a God whose design on history and whose kingdom cannot be frustrated by our propensity to fail. At the same time, we must acknowledge our capacity for failure. Just as the men of Reserve Battalion 101 were caught up in the culture around them and became willing agents of evil, so, too, must we question the assumptions our culture inculcates within us. Rather than disengage, we must serve the world humbly and prayerfully, questioning our motivations and methods, knowing that the story is not about us. This is God's story, and he will use it for his own glory.

Secondly, as history leads us to our own depravity, we must begin to build a society that promotes justice and serves to counter the disintegration of social order that enables atrocities such as the Holocaust. Snyder takes up this lesson at the end of his manuscript, drawing out a powerful and practical message from the Holocaust:

> Most of us would like to think that we possess . . . 'moral instinct' and 'human goodness.' Perhaps we imagine that we would be rescuers in some future catastrophe. Yet if states were destroyed, local institutions corrupted, and economic incentives directed towards murder, few of us would behave well. There is little reason to think that we are ethically superior to the Europeans of the 1930s and 1940s, or for that matter less vulnerable to the kind of ideas that Hitler so successfully promulgated and realized. If we are serious about emulating rescuers, we should build in advance the structures that make it more likely that we would do so. Rescue, in this broad sense, thus requires a firm grasp of the ideas that challenged conventional politics and opened the way to an unprecedented crime.[9]

As we see the collapse of society and those other events that enabled the Holocaust, we must learn to create societies that forestall such occurrences.

We must be concerned with more than producing societal bulwarks against mass violence. History should call us to examine ourselves to prevent the murderous, evil tendencies present within us all. In his undergraduate text on genocide studies, noted scholar Adam Jones provides a concise recommendation (among others) for preventing further episodes of mass violence in the world: "There is a critical individual dimension. . . . Each person must monitor, as objectively as possible, the tendency to hatred

9. Snyder, *Black Earth*, 320–21.

and exclusivism that is present in us all. This temptation always exists to believe *we* are superior and right—whether we bolster this with religious belief, a secular stance, or a mix of the two."[10] This is a lesson that Christians could stand to learn. How many American Christians were quick to champion the 2003 invasion of Iraq, oblivious to the effects it would have on that country and its citizens? How quick are we to advocate war in the name of our own security without questioning the effects it will have on literally millions of others? In this sense, we have repeated the same logic as the Nazis. To be secure, we assume we must destroy the Other, a necessary price that we must pay to be safe. But is this the way of our savior? As we look to the past and behold the wicked inclinations of the human heart, we need to draw our own hearts to the prince of peace, to fill them with the values of his kingdom, and to draw ourselves away from the world.

Here, the sacrament of confession, lost to most Protestant churches, is quite helpful. When we confess our sins to one another, especially as we draw those confessions inward and focus on the sins of the heart, through God's grace, we begin to rid ourselves of such tendencies. In this regard, then, history should call us to confession and revive within the church the need for some form of public confession—whether through the clergy, an accountability partner, or a small group. We will take this up in greater detail in the next chapter. It is important, however, to recognize that history reveals our depravity, but should not leave us lamenting it. Rather, we must confess, privately and publically, and in so doing challenge the structures of oppression, destruction, and evil in our own time.

This leads us into the last concept that we can learn as we see our depravity in history. Learning of our own sinfulness and seeing such capabilities in others should not cause us to despair but rather point us toward our savior. The angel of history gapes as it falls forward, seeking meaning, searching for direction. As the chaos abounds around, as empires clash and fall, as populations are wiped off the earth, and as the story of humanity unravels into

10. Jones, *Genocide*, 401–402.

the very fires of hell, we see the vanity of our own pursuits. Left to our own devices, we stumble. We put Hitlers in positions of power, we destroy the creation over which we were called to steward. But in the midst of the darkness, God calls us. We do well to remember that "every shock of history is *a* day of the Lord foreshadowing *the* day of the Lord, because history whispers ultimacy."[11] For the Christian, studying the past, especially as we behold our own potential for depravity reflected in the human story, should point us toward the future, to the day when we will stand before the Lord of history to face judgment—the day on which the wrath of God, which we have gained glimpses of during the temporal span of human history, will be on full display.

Lest this awareness of our own sinfulness and coming judgment as we look through the lens of history be reduced to a mere harbinger of gloom and doom, rejoice! Yes, we are Adam's fallen children, prone to wander from our birth. But while a healthy degree of sorrow and repentance is called for (2 Cor 7:10), this is not the end of the story. As we see the wickedness of humanity through its tired story and the evil that is indelibly stamped on our own hearts, it should point us to our need for a savior. Thus, when we see the darkness of the human experience, when we see Benjamin's angel of history faltering backwards into chaos, it should cause us to look to Christ, our deliverer and our hope.

CONCLUSION

Benjamin's angel of history cannot grasp the debris that grows around it. The angel tries in vain to pause, to put together the fragmented pieces of the past to fix the catastrophe of the present. If the angel could but pause and learn, perhaps that which is around him could be made whole. This is the task of the Christian as he or she looks to the past. The world looks to history and sees chaos. There is disorder, violence, and civilization after civilization rising and falling with no change in the human condition. Those without

11. Ortlund, *Isaiah*, 126.

Christ turn to the past and try to frame a lesson based on human strength. Perhaps, they reason, if we look at an event like the Holocaust, and study its nuances, we can avoid another Holocaust. This is the danger of putting man in the driving seat of history. When we try to learn a human lesson from the past, when we see history through the lens of postmodern thought, our lessons come up short. Man is prone to weakness, prone to failure. Even those among us who like to assure ourselves that were we born in a different time, were we alive during the Holocaust, for example, we would have been among those who chose to resist evil, find that our best efforts are frustrated. As we use the past to mediate our present, as we absolve ourselves of the sins we commit in our own time by saying we would have stood against the sins of a previous generation, we hopelessly fool ourselves by placing ourselves on a non-existent moral pedestal.

This is why it is so crucial to have a Christ-centered hermeneutic through which we can read the past. This is why we must first acknowledge and grasp and rejoice in the sovereignty of a transcendent God who willfully reveals himself to us through the created order, a God who entered into the very process of history as a man. With the foundation we began to lay in the second chapter, we can begin to see that history does indeed have a lesson. This lesson is not anthrocentric, for history itself is not our story, but rather tells the tale of the divine, reveals his majesty, and forces us to see our utter depravity and proclivity toward evil. As we see ourselves in the evil of the past, as the face of the guard at Auschwitz or the slave master rather than in the person who chose to rescue Jews and slaves, we begin to get a sense of our own need for a savior. This lends us to a stronger moral formation in the present as we begin to question the ways in which we have compromised with evil in our own time and drives us back into the hands of a savior. History, then, becomes another means of revelation and teaches us of our need for God, slowly calling us back to him as he works out his purposes throughout time and space.

5

The Redemptive Value of the Past: Dealing with the Skeletons in our Closet

"Remembering is never a quiet act of introspection or retrospection. It is a painful re-membering, a putting together of the dismembered past to make sense of the trauma of the present."[1]

"Forgiving is not forgetting; it's actually remembering—remembering and not using your right to hit back. It's a second chance for a new beginning. And the remembering part is particularly important."[2]

"Both we and our fathers have sinned; we have committed iniquity; we have done wickedness." (Ps 106:6)

ADRIAAN SMUTS PRESENTED HIS story as a matter of fact: "I'm sorry that people were hurt as a result of our actions and that people had to be killed in the process, but you must realize that in a war people get killed on both sides and hurt on both sides."[3]

1. Bhabha, *Location of Culture*, 215.
2. Tutu and Tutu, *Book of Forgiving*, 37.
3. Smuts, "Amnesty Application."

Smuts, who lived in Richards Bay, South Africa, was a member of the *Afrikaner Weerstandsbeweging*—the Afrikaner Resistance Movement (AWB)—a white-nationalist organization that supported the continuation of apartheid government in South Africa. Deeply committed to his cause, Smuts and several others became convinced that preserving white dominance in South Africa was a necessary aim, regardless of the costs.

Upon hearing erroneous reports that blacks had attacked whites at a beach in nearby Durban, Smuts and two of his associates decided to act upon their beliefs. As Smuts later recalled, the group traveled to Durban to carry out an assault designed not to exact revenge but rather to draw attention to what he and his friends believed to be government indifference toward attacks on whites in the country. Smuts and the others originally planned on following a taxi with black riders and attacking the vehicle's inhabitants; however, the taxi turned off the main road and into a populated area in which such an assault would be impossible. The group then decided to pursue a bus full of black passengers. This time they followed through with their plan, killing seven of the riders and injuring twenty-seven others.

The attack was one of many such incidents during the apartheid era in South Africa. Like Smuts, the testimony given by numerous perpetrators of these crimes are striking for the level of indifference expressed by the criminals. More chilling is the way in which Smuts and many others drew connections between their murderous actions and their Christian faith. Testifying as part of his application for amnesty, Smuts recalled that, "I was raised in a conservative home. We were a religious family and we believed in a triune God. From a very early age onwards I attended political meetings with my father. And as a result of that, my objectives became the following—I believed also that these objectives were very important to me. I believed in the triune God, in the preservation and continued existence of the Afrikaans language and culture, self-determination, and the continued existence of the Boer people in its own territory. The promotion of an independent

Christian freedom at all costs."[4] Smuts perceived Christianity and whiteness to be coterminous and felt morally compelled to protect both at all costs.

Smuts presented his testimony as part of South Africa's Truth and Reconciliation Commission, the brainchild of a joint effort between the country's post-apartheid civic and religious leaders. The commission operated on the premise of restorative justice, holding that for South Africa to heal as a nation from the wounds of nearly half a century of apartheid, the truth of past atrocities needed to come to light at the national level, and that forgiveness (legal and otherwise) and reconciliation needed to accompany these confessions. Persons who committed certain violent crimes under the apartheid system were offered amnesty in exchange for a public confession of the details of their crimes as well as a sincerely offered apology to the victims and/or surviving family members. The sessions were emotional, and often those with blood on their hands met face-to-face with mothers, brothers, friends, and other close associates of persons they had murdered.[5]

While South Africa's Truth and Reconciliation Committees were far from perfect and have been subject to a fair degree of criticism over the past two decades, they do have much to teach us about the Christian necessity for engaging history. Many nations seek to brush the darker periods of their past under the rug, to craft a historical narrative that paints the nation in a better light. We in the United States are particularly guilty of this. Similarly, there is a reluctance in the church to address past sins that have been committed in the name of God. South Africa, however, chose the route of redemption, opting for public confessions of crimes committed during the apartheid era in an effort toward national repentance and reconciliation.

In chapter three, we talked about the ways in which historical narrative empowers the voice of those who have suffered. History, properly used, can be the megaphone of the silenced, a chance to

4. Smuts, "Amnesty Application."

5. In Smuts's case, the families of those killed in the attack were opposed to the granting of amnesty.

heal for the victim, and a channel of redress for the wronged. In this chapter, we will consider the other side of this coin to reveal why history is important for those who stand as the heirs and benefactors of the oppressive systems of the past. Americans who engage history from a Christ-centered perspective will find that, for us, the past is a call to repentance, a chance to beg forgiveness for the sins of our fathers, and an opportunity to make right the wrongs of those who went before us by pursuing justice in the present. For the Christian, then, history has a redemptive value, and any Christian approach to history must amplify the ongoing need for repentance we face as a church, as a nation, and as individuals.

COLLECTIVE GUILT AND HISTORICAL REDEMPTION

Contemporary Christianity has lost sight of the Bible's teaching on corporate guilt. The evangelical movement of the past century has emphasized the doctrine of repentance on the individual level, promoting alter calls and preaching a message of born-again conversion. A biblical understanding of repentance, however, focuses not only on the self but also calls for collective repentance by the nation and God's elect. As we take a redemptive approach to history, we must consider repentance at the national, church, and individual level.

There is a strong biblical argument to be made for corporate repentance. Many of the Psalms are songs of repentance in which the Psalmist calls the nation to repent. In Psalm 106, the author states that "both we and our fathers have sinned," establishing the principle that guilt can be shared on the national level across generations. The prophets devoted a good portion of their respective ministries to calling for national repentance, for a corporate acknowledgement of guilt, and a return to the ways of the Lord. Ezra and Nehemiah called the returning exiles to repent of the sins committed by their fathers that resulted in the nation being cast out of the holy land in the first place. In his famous condemnation of the Pharisees, Christ admonished Palestine's religious elite for their complicity in their ancestors' murderous actions toward God's messengers: "Woe to you, scribes and Pharisees, hypocrites! For you build the tombs of the prophets, and decorate the monuments of the righteous, saying, 'If we had lived in the days of our fathers, we would not have taken part with them in shedding the blood of the prophets.' Thus you witness against yourselves that you are sons of those who murdered the prophets" (Matt 23:29–31). These scriptures, together with the rest of the biblical witness, attest to the fact that guilt can be shared corporately and across generations, as can confession and repentance.

These principles have strong resonance today. Some countries have done an excellent, or at least passable, job addressing the sinful periods of their history. South Africa's commitment to national repentance and renewal embodied in the Truth and Reconciliation Commissions is an example of this. The commissions provided an avenue through which the guilty were offered the chance of repentance and readmittance into society in the new post-apartheid South Africa, and victims and their families were offered a chance to forgive, allowing for their memories to slowly heal. While the Truth and Reconciliation Commissions failed to completely erase the legacies of apartheid and racial problems persist in South Africa, they became a vehicle through which the nation confessed its sins, repented, and began to construct a new reality.

Nations are often forced to reconcile with their pasts through defeat in war or other major national upheavals. South Africa's need for repentance was brought about through the decisive collapse of apartheid through international pressure and a global boycott, divestment, and sanctions movement targeted at the apartheid government. Germany was forced to confront the horrors of the Nazi regime, especially the Holocaust, following the country's defeat in World War II. The decisiveness of that defeat brought Germany to its knees, and the subsequent trials that targeted many of the Holocaust's perpetrators forced a national conversation about what went wrong and how to deal with the legacies of the Holocaust, as most German citizens were, in some fashion, complicit in its horrors.

The United States has never dealt with such a massive defeat. To a degree, the Civil War did, at least temporarily, force a conversation on America's original sin of racism. This conversation continued through the period of Reconstruction (1865–1877)[6]; however, the sin of racism had already worked itself deeply into the American system, and the attempt at national reconciliation and redress for black Americans envisioned by Reconstruction gave way to a revived racist power base in the United States that resulted in a *de facto* return to slavery for many blacks in America that persisted into the twentieth and twenty-first centuries. Recent events—including but certainly not limited to the shooting of black Americans such as Travon Martin, Michael Brown, and Tamir Rice, the racialized nature of the war on drugs, and the inherently racially biased prison industrial complex—have revealed that America has not yet repented of its original sin, nor is there anything close to a national willingness to engage in a discussion about the persistence of racial injustice in American history.

In the face of continued racial disparities in America, our country still has yet to have a significant national conversation about our past and present injustices. When we do talk about our country's racial history, we focus on the triumphs, not the original injustices themselves or the continued legacies of those injustices. We promote figures like Harriet Tubman for her bravery and tenacity in challenging slavery, as if these characteristics could be mapped onto America as a whole, rather than acknowledging the horrors of race-based slavery that were enshrined into our very constitution and national life from the beginning, necessitating her resistance. We preach a triumphalist narrative of Civil Rights

6. There are ongoing historiographic debates about the legacy and meaning of Reconstruction; however, there is a growing consensus that this period of American history represented a radical democratic experiment in which the racial shortcomings of America's original founding were sought to be countered. This stands in contrast with the traditional view that Reconstruction represented a period of excess on the part of radical Republicans, which led to an inevitable backlash in the Compromise of 1877. I concur with the former, and find Reconstruction to be an ambitious, though ultimately doomed, attempt at correcting America's original sin of racism.

in the twentieth century, arguing that America, the promised land, always found a way to become better, to grow, all the while obfuscating the ongoing need to work for justice for black Americans. We whitewash the legacy of visionaries like Rosa Parks and Martin Luther King Jr., touting them as representatives of American values, ignoring the powerful critiques of the American system itself they offered along the way. We engage with history when it is convenient, when it is self-laudatory, but we ignore the many skeletons in our closet. All of this serves to blind us to the contemporary realities of inequality and injustice present within our society which have manifested themselves through our nearly two-and-a-half centuries of national life. There is an urgent need for a humble rethinking of the American national narrative. Like South Africa, we need to have a moment of national reckoning—of confession, redemption, and reconciliation—to come to terms with our dark past and with our present and to begin to rework the legacies of our troubled history.

Here is a call for American Christians to engage the past. The church should be at the forefront of challenging the persistence of racism in American society, and history provides a channel through which to accomplish this. The church must become historical in its thinking, to incorporate discussions of America's embrace of racism throughout its history into our gatherings, to draw attention to that history among its members, and to then spread that knowledge to others. The church can publically confess the sins of the nation, crying out to God for forgiveness. Further, the church can serve as a conscience to the state as it actively disrupts ongoing injustices being committed by the nation.[7]

This draws our attention to the second level at which history can be redemptive. There is an urgent need for the church

---

7. The growing sanctuary church movement, wherein churches provide sanctuary for undocumented immigrants, is a powerful example of this and an example of a practical way in which a Christ-centered understanding of history can be a call to repentance and action in the present. One could also cite the rising support for the Boycott, Divestment, and Sanctions movement for Palestinian rights that has been embraced by a growing number of denominations.

to corporately confess the sins of its own past. Many of the grave sins committed by America and other western nations first found support within the walls of the church. Slavery, a sin embedded in America's founding that has left legacies across the span of American history, was preached as an unqualified good from pulpits throughout antebellum America, and not just in the South. Proslavery pastors and congregations touted the Bible's support for slavery in both testaments without acknowledging the difference between the institution in Hebrew and Roman society and how slavery functioned in the transatlantic system. Apologists for slavery stripped verses of their context to support their case. Pastors expounded the Hamitic myth, claiming that the curse Noah placed on his son Ham applied to all Africans, who were taken to be the descendants of Ham. In the Genesis passage, after Ham "saw the nakedness of his father and told his two brothers outside" (Gen 9:22), Noah admonished Ham, cursing him and his descendants to be "a servant of servants to his brothers" (Gen 9:25). In this obscure passage, antebellum Christians claimed divine sanction for the abusive nature of American slavery.

The church in America has continued to provide cover for America's original sin. Many evangelical congregations vehemently supported segregation and opposed integration throughout the first half of the twentieth century. In the second half of the twentieth century, evangelicals increasingly refused to send their children to integrated schools, opting instead for the establishment of private schools that catered primarily to white students. In the past decade, the silence of white-majority churches in the face of increased racial injustice and a revived white power movement has spoken volumes about its priorities. The American church has been complicit in America's national sin. A reckoning of this history needs to be made. The church in America must publically confess this sin, and history provides the clarion call for repentance.

As a first step, we as believers must begin to challenge racism within our midst. I often pose the question to my students as to what was the most segregated time in American history. Many guess the years immediately preceding the Civil War. Others draw attention to the Jim Crow period that followed Reconstruction. Yet neither of these answers is correct. The most racially segregated time in American history is 10:30 in the morning on any given Sunday. From the arrival of the first African slaves in the area that was to become the United States in the seventeenth century, white Christianity has actively sought to distance itself from black Christians. America's first churches were segregated, and this gulf persists today. Financially, we disproportionately devote our resources to the white church. We rarely elevate our black brothers and sisters to positions of influence or leadership. If we as a believing community have any hope of leading an effort at national reconciliation and repentance, we must first begin to look within the four walls of our churches, to clean the inside of the cup first so that we may then clean the outside.

Historically, the church in America and throughout the rest of the world has sinned, and it is our duty as Christians to confess and repent of the sins of our fathers. The crusades, Indian removal, church support for antisemitism and the Holocaust, attacks on immigrants, and demonizing, marginalizing, and inflicting violence on LGBTQI+ persons have all left a dark stain on the body. There is a grave need for the church to acknowledge this, to yield to history as a powerful agent for redemption within the body of Christ. As we participate in this process, we glorify God.

Yet mere confession of our misdeeds is not enough. Biblical redemption assumes repentance, which demands true and lasting change. Writing on the need to challenge racism and other forms of oppression within our midst and regaining a sense of Christian community that cuts across markers of identity, social activist Paul Ricketts observes that "in dismantling these stumbling blocks, we must tap into the power of the Spirit while acknowledging the truth that structural oppression and systemic racism does spiritual violence to us all. To be faithful in this time, we must do more than admit that such oppression and attitudes of privilege exist. We must fully act to eliminate them if we wish to be fully inclusive in ways that are more than mere words."[8] Empowered by the

8. See Ricketts, "Move in our Midst."

Spirit, emboldened by a God-centered quest for justice, we must make changes.[9] Those of us in the white church must be willing to listen to our brothers and sisters of color, to yield to their voices, and to let go of our firm grasp on power. As we do so, we must be careful to not assert our own voice or narrative too strongly; rather, we must submit ourselves to the wishes, experiences, and recommendations of those whom we have marginalized. Only then can we begin to hope for a truly productive conversation and for reconciliation among the body of Christ. Through this unity, this mutual love and respect, we will make Christ known to the nations (1 John 4:7–11).

Redemption at the corporate level, especially the nation and the church, is one of the principle benefits Christians can derive from engaging with history, but there is also a call for individual redemption within the study of the past. South Africa's Truth and Reconciliation Commissions demonstrate the ways in which individual confession (and, in some cases, repentance) can contribute to national restoration, redemption, and reconciliation. As we study the past, we need to begin to understand our own role within it. We must fit ourselves and our own personal histories within the narratives of the national and religious communities to which we belong.

This is where the study of one's family history can transition from being a mere hobby to satisfy personal curiosity into an act of confession and repentance. The past several decades have seen a significant increase in interest in reconstructing family trees, with

9. One of the greatest challenges preventing Americans, Christian or otherwise, from actively participating in this work is that we have convinced ourselves that we are not racists by focusing on explicit, intentional acts of racism as the only definition of racism. Therefore, people believe that if they do not join the Klu Klux Klan or express an outwardly hostile attitude toward persons of color, then they are guiltless. But if we examine the history of racism in the United States, we find that it works more powerfully on a systemic level and does not always carry with it explicit intent (segregated housing patterns, as prevalent today as at any point in American history, are but one example of this). Here, there is a necessity for those like myself who are in the white majority to admit our incidental role in reifying racial disparities within national life and to join those movements aimed at tackling these broad issues.

many services, such as Ancestry.com, facilitating the construction of family histories. We often trace our family trees hoping to learn about the nobility of our ancestors, yet what shadows exist in our own familial closets? How do we respond to ancestors who may have been slave holders? Our ancestors who fought for the Confederacy to defend the institution of slavery? Have our families benefited from living on land taken from America's first inhabitants? As Christians, we need to be careful when viewing our family history that we don't read the values and narrative of the nation back into our own story. Individuals often do this when lauding ancestors who were war heroes without assessing the morality or immorality of the wars in which these soldiers fought. We must openly acknowledge the faults of our mothers and fathers. After all, as Israel told its history time and again throughout the pages of scripture, Abraham's acquiescing to Sarah's demands that he have a child through her servant was recounted (Gen 16:2), as was Moses' obstinate striking of the rock that barred his entrance to the promised land (Num 20:11–12), the slaughter of the righteous Zechariah (2 Chr 24:20–21), along with the sins of scores of others. We have sinned with our fathers, and we must acknowledge this and repent.

History serves a redemptive purpose at the individual level when it allows those of us who are the beneficiaries of the legacies of oppression within American history to see and challenge our own privilege within society. History has the potential to elevate the voices of the oppressed; it also provides an occasion for the oppressor to examine himself, to search the ways in which he has become a respecter of persons (Rom 2:11), and to challenge those assumptions in the present. Invariably, when I have this conversation with my students, one will raise his or her hand and declare: "This doesn't apply to me. My ancestors came to America in the twentieth century, long after Indian removal and slavery." Yet we as individuals are heirs to the legacies of these processes and continue to derive the economic and cultural benefits created by these institutions. We must acknowledge and confess this intersection between our individual privilege resulting from injustice and the sins of the nation itself.

NARRATIVE AND PRAXIS: HOW CAN THE PAST BE USED REDEMPTIVELY?

Starting a national conversation about the skeletons in America's closet is a daunting task. Where does such a conversation begin? Who should be leading it? Such national conversations typically take place in the wake of loss in war or otherwise, but America is not on the edge of such a defeat. If anything, we remain ascendant, firmly fixed, at least for the moment, in a position of power and prestige. There is nothing that is forcing a reworking of our narrative.

Christians can begin by challenging the historical mythologies that place our respective nation states, churches, and personal histories on a pedestal. There is an impulsive tendency among Americans—and American Christians in particular—that fosters an instantaneously defensive posture whenever the innate goodness of America or the church is challenged. There is a great need for a renewed sense of humility, for an open willingness to confess our sins as a nation, as a church, and as individuals, to bring the skeletons in our closet out into the open. We must not fear to admit that the church has sinned, that the nation has sinned, and that we, as individuals, share this collective guilt. We must be open about our past, and we must work this act of confession into our corporate existence. This process can be facilitated by reworking our corporate narratives, engaging in the process of reconfiguring historical space, and the pursuit of justice in the present that offers redress for historical wrongs.

Over the past years, I have had the privilege and honor to volunteer with Musalaha, a Jerusalem-based organization that facilitates a biblical model of reconciliation between Jews and Arabs in the Holy Land. As anyone with even an ounce of familiarity with the conflict in Palestine can imagine, this work is difficult. Each side claims that it has been historically wronged over the twentieth century, and each side appeals to its historical narrative to advance its agenda in the present. As Musalaha brings people on both sides of the conflict together, there is little agreement as to what the "real" history is, and both sides cling to their respective narratives.

This is not unlike our situation here in the United States, although we perhaps do not often acknowledge the deep conflicts that are present within our society. As individuals and groups, we often hold firmly to the narratives that reinforce our beliefs, refusing to understand the narrative of the Other. Narrative, and particularly historical narrative, is what grounds our identity, what secures our position in society. Yet how do we, as persons of faith, engage history redemptively in the context of so many competing narratives? In their curriculum on reconciliation, Musalaha suggests the following as a first step: "Bridge the narratives as much as possible . . . there are many difficulties that stand in the way of completely bridging the gap between the . . . opposing narratives. But this cannot and should not keep us from trying to narrow the gap as much as possible. This can be done in a number of ways: by focusing on shared history in the area of social and cultural history, and by constantly challenging our own narrative."[10] While it may seem impossible, we must seek to build a bridge, to establish a point of connection, between the competing historical narratives that complicate the achievement of justice in our society. This can be facilitated through developing a joint narrative grounded not in political or ethnic identities but on a shared cultural and national legacy that transcends the difference of narrative. Crafting a joint narrative, however, requires that we first spend time listening to those whose experiences differ markedly from our own. We must expand our social and ecclesial circles to include perspectives that radically challenge our own.

Bridging narratives, however, can only go so far. Musalaha's curriculum goes on to explain that "we can try and understand each other's narrative" as "an essential step towards reconciliation, for while we may never totally agree on the past, if we understand

10. "History and Narrative."

each other's narratives, we will be able to understand each other better, and develop empathy for each other."[11] Understanding the narrative of those who disagree with us fosters national reconciliation and redemption through engendering empathy and making it more difficult for hate to take root. This is often where reconciliation efforts collapse, for it requires not just an intellectual ascent to the narrative of the Other but also an acceptance of its validity. Musalaha's curriculum states that moving beyond mere understanding, "we must also accept the other narrative. This does not mean that we must agree with it, but we must accept it as valid, and respect the importance it holds for the other side. As we accept and respect each other's narratives, we also feel acceptance and respect towards our own narrative, since it is a mutually beneficial process that moves in two directions. In this sense, our identity is affirmed and a way for reconciliation is prepared."[12] The understanding and acceptance of narratives that challenge our own becomes the way through which history becomes redemptive, healing the wounds within the hearts of those who have suffered historical and contemporary injustice *and* cleansing and releasing the heart of those who have been the oppressor.

There is a word of caution that is necessary here. Learning to understand and accept narratives that challenge our own does not necessitate moral agreement with them. It would be wrong to suggest that those who have suffered some of the greatest abuse across the span of American history would have to ascent to the moral legitimacy of the narrative of those who oppressed them. This was one of the critiques leveled against South Africa's Truth and Reconciliation Commission. Detractors claimed that the process of granting clemency to those who confessed legitimized the crimes that had been committed during apartheid. We must bridge the divide between narratives, learning to accept the narrative of those different from us, but we must also maintain a firm sense of right and wrong, an acknowledgement that certain narratives carry with them a greater moral legitimacy than others, and to correct, in

11. "History and Narrative."
12. "History and Narrative."

tangible ways, the injustices perpetrated throughout our national history. This is a messy process, but a necessary one if we are to ground our study of the past in a gospel-centered perspective. It is a thoroughly biblical one in that the vertical reconciliation between God and man achieved at the cross necessitates our horizontal reconciliation with our fellow human beings (Eph 2:14–16).

In addition to bridging the narrative gap, the past can also be used redemptively by reconfiguring historic space as a means of challenging national mythologies. The sacred spaces of the nation, the White House, Arlington National Cemetery, Civil War battlefields, historic plantations in the America South, and countless others are public venues for presenting and mythologizing the national past. Most of these landmarks are conceived in such a way as to present the dominant narrative of the United States as a benevolent nation, a city on a hill. Is there room for the presentation of other narratives within these historic spaces? Can we acknowledge the role of slaves in building the White House, our icon of democracy, and thus publically confess the sin of slavery that developed along with our democracy? Can we honor the lives lost who lay at rest in Arlington Cemetery while also commemorating the countless lives lost by our so-called enemies in Vietnam, Korea, Iraq, and elsewhere? By joining other narratives to the dominant national narrative within our historic spaces, we need not erase the history of good and positive accomplishments that is present in many of these landmarks, but we can begin to embrace the different, complex, and yet overlapping narratives that are part of our national history. This, too, is an important step toward a redemptive use of the past.

Finally, the past can be redemptive as it leads to change in the present. As we unpack the skeletons in our closet at the national, church, and individual level, this process must inform questions of injustice affecting society now. There will come a point at which the present becomes the past, when the angel of history is blown beyond our own times and steadily into the future. What will future generations of historians write about our times? What practices will they condemn? Will we be written about as a nation, a church, and individuals who continued long processes of historical injustice, or will we be, by God's grace, those who participate in the outworking of justice, those who build the ideals of the kingdom in the present, looking forward to their future realization in the glory to come? We can begin to embrace history as a means of redemption by translating our confession of past sins into present action, through not just acknowledging and bemoaning the sins of those who came before us, but repenting of their sins and embracing holiness, righteousness, and justice in our own time.

CONCLUSION

The tragic 2015 killing of nine black members of the Emanuel African Methodist Episcopal Church in Charleston, South Carolina by white supremacist Dylan Roof, which came after a series of killings of black Americans by white police officers, forced America, at least for a time, to confront its historical sins and the racism that remains as a legacy of those sins. A contentious facet of these debates centered on the role of the Confederacy in the American national narrative, especially the role of monuments to heroes of the Confederacy. Shortly after the Charleston shooting, activist Bree Newsome climbed the flagpole outside of the South Carolina statehouse and removed the Confederate flag in a symbolic act of defiance. Her action called a nation to stop lionizing the architects of slavery, to repent of the sins of our fathers, and to build a world in which the perpetuation of those sins is unimaginable.

This is not to say that we must erase the painful chapters of our national history. Rather, we must learn to use the past redemptively, to critique the treatment of figures like Robert E. Lee, Andrew Jackson, and even Thomas Jefferson (who not only owned slaves, but raped at least one of them, Sally Hemmings) as heroes, emblems of the best our nation has to offer. Such figures should remind us of how far America has strayed from its own ideals, and, more importantly, from biblical ideals. The past is a powerful agent of sanctification when properly understood and used. We, together with our fathers, have sinned. We must uncover their sins, repent of them at all levels, and move forward with a new agenda of justice. As believers, those who bear the name and image of Christ and his kingdom, we must become his ambassadors, to correct the faults of our fathers. The past has the ability to call us into this repentance, therefore, we must engage it humbly and with an eye toward our own times.

We must not be armchair historians, erudite individuals with a head-knowledge of the past who are content to treat history as a mere intellectual curiosity. History must propel us to action. We must not rely on the tired narratives of past generations that seek to exalt our own glory and achievements, but we must be willing to submit to narratives that challenge our own, that make us uncomfortable. For years, the unofficial motto of the history department in which I now teach part time was: "We are the department that makes you feel uncomfortable." Discomfort can be good when it leads us to change, and this is yet a further reason why Christians must care about the past, must engage history.

This again points to the need for Christians to make history a regular part of their lives. It is challenging enough for us to uncover the sins that inhabit our private world. But in a context of increased political, racial, and religious tribalization at the global level, Christians are ill-disposed to challenge the corporate sins that afflict our national and religious communities or to repent of the ways in which we as individuals join in their sins. As history becomes the mirror in which our depravity is reflected back to us, it also has the power to expose our collective sins. When we allow the past to speak to us in this way, and when we respond to its rebuke with repentance, the redemptive power of history accomplishes its purpose.

6

Militant Nostalgism:
The Dangers of the Past

"Myth deprives the object of which it speaks of all History. In it, history evaporates. It is a kind of ideal servant: it prepares all things, brings them, lays them out, the master arrives, it silently disappears: all that is left for one to do is to enjoy this beautiful object without wondering where it comes from. Or even better: it can only come from eternity."[1]

"The present times always appear to be peculiarly dangerous, because they are nearest to our anxious gaze, and whatever evils are rife are sure to be observed, while the faults of past ages are further off, and are more easily overlooked."[2]

"Say not, 'Why were the former days better than these?' For it is not from wisdom that you ask this." (Eccl 7:10)

AMERICA LONGS FOR MAYBERRY, the fictionalized small-town in which the 1960s feel-good comedy *The Andy Griffith Show* was set. The town evokes the quietude of simpler times, the cultural motif

1. Barthes, *Mythologies*, 151.
2. Spurgeon, *Treasury of David*, 141.

of the nuclear family, and a place and era in which life proceeded at a slower pace. Mayberry had no cell phones, no social media, and none of the entanglements of contemporary life that have entrapped most Americans, yet on which they rely for their daily lives. Mayberry existed in an apolitical state, with no discussion of racial tensions, women's equality, or the sufferings experienced by millions of Americans whose lives were not reflected on the small screen. If only we could return to Mayberry, to celebrate a simple life, to slow down the rat race of contemporary American life that leaves many feeling void of connection to community, country, and God.

The problem with this longing is that Mayberry is fictional. The show obscures reality. America in the 1960s was characterized by racism, sexism, growing income inequality, and an environmental crises brought on by nearly a century of industrialization and unbridled capitalism. Mayberry presents a very narrow picture, an aberration rather than the norm. Communities like Watts in Los Angeles, the Hough in Cleveland, and the impoverished region of Appalachia belie the fallacy of the image of Mayberry. Mayberry swallows reality whole, replacing it with a picture of privilege and exclusion, a world only accessible to a narrow few. Mayberry is the myth of American history, an idol of the past demanding our homage in the present.

I cringe whenever I hear my brothers and sisters in Christ, especially those of an older generation but increasingly those of a younger one as well, long to return to the "simpler" times of the past. The representation of America found in shows like *Andy Griffin* (and others such as *Little House on the Prairie* or *The Waltons*) obfuscates the reality of history, forcing us to an escapist mentality vis-à-vis the troubles of our own times as we long pine for a world that did not exist. In the face of this escapist culture, it is worth asking precisely what is the history to which some long to return? The past is a darker place than our collective memory recalls. Do we wish to relocate ourselves to an era in American history when professing Christians journeyed straight from church on Sunday morning to witness the lynching of persons of color, or to a time and place in which women were objects forced into the idolatry of domesticity in the name of Christian honor? In contemporary society, a longing for the halcyon days of old is often code-speak for angst about the increasing diversity that characterizes American society and the gradual, though slow, push for equality for women that threatens too many a contemporary male ego. The church must loudly and categorically stand against such appeals and seek to actively, intentionally, and without abandon engage the times in which we live.

The idol of Mayberry stands before us all and demands our worship. The past is a dangerous object for one to possess, and we must remain cognizant of its risks. We have covered in previous chapters that history illuminates our depravity and that studying the darker episodes of our corporate and individual histories can call us to repentance. But there is a persistent threat facing the angel of history as it plods along through the storm. Just as we often imagine ourselves in heroic roles in the past, ignoring our own potential for sin, we also idolize the past, mythologizing the world in which our fathers and mothers lived. Our goal in this chapter will be to counter this thread of nefarious nostalgia and explore the ways in which embracing a false narrative of history can be poisonous to our faith and society in the present.

THE COMMODIFICATION OF THE NOSTALGIC

The first two decades of the twentieth century have seen the rise of a curious trend that has profound ramifications for how Christians engage the past. Amidst the rise of a wired culture in which it is impossible to separate the online world from the real one, disruptive patterns in communities that are altering the social structures that once anchored individuals within groups, and a rancorous political culture that privileges a narrative of crisis, a militant nostalgism has captured the cultural imagination of America with a call to return to a time and place in which this interminable societal ennui is erased.

Nostalgia has become commodified, giving birth to an industry of its own. The proliferation of sales of DVDs of old TV shows, the rise of networks like TV Land in which reruns of the "classics" draw viewers deep into a mythology of America's cultural past, the "rebooting" of television classics, and ballads promoting the virtues of an America long-gone yet not quite fully out of grasp have become big business. The emergence of nostalgia as a cultural phenomenon embraces a simple message: the past is better, the past is safe. The world was knowable back then, morality was clear cut, and the evils of our contemporary world were unknown.

This nostalgia is not necessarily anything new. The revolutionary 1970s sitcom *All in the Family* opened with lyrics that wistfully speak of the past. While the content of the show was a direct challenge to this notion and a call to come to grips with the changing times, the show's main character, Archie Bunker, remained fixed in the world of his pre-World War II youth. The rising inflation of the 1970s, the open and obvious racial tension, America's changing role and image in the world, all seemed foreign and dangerous to the aging man, and the pace of change was often more than he could bear. If Archie could have his way, he would return to the world that seemed to be vanishing around him.

We are trapped in a world of nostalgia. We long for the past, for a certainty in which to anchor our scattered present. Like the angel of history, we gaze at the rubbish heap of history laid at our feet. We feel helpless, knowing that the incessant storm termed progress pushes us unwillingly forward into the present. We long, perhaps paradoxically, for something new *and* something old, a change of our present by returning to our imagined past. We are yearning to fill a void, to even understand what causes our void, and we seek to find our contentment in familiar terrain.

HISTORICAL ILLITERACY, ESCAPISM, AND THE KINGDOM OF GOD

What is it about the past that evokes this powerful desire? Why do we long for a world that has passed before us? Is there necessarily anything wrong with desiring to return to "simpler" times? In Proverbs, Solomon admonishes the wise that, "Like a dog that returns to his vomit is a fool who repeats his folly" (Prov 26:11). Contemporary Americans—and here Christians are as guilty as their secular counterparts—cling to militant nostalgism out of a lack of knowledge of the past, a desire to cling to our often-vanishing sense of power and entitlement as we live in a changing world, discontent in our own lives, and a desire to escape from the demands of kingdom life in the present. All of these disrupt our spiritual growth, belie the need for a Christ-centered engagement with the past, and demand renewed commitment to the future.

Americans are woefully ignorant about the past, and our current model of social science curriculum seems unlikely to solve the issue any time soon. Increased historical literacy can serve as a corrective to the dangerous tendency to romanticize the past. This is part of what is at stake in a redemptive use of the past as discussed in the previous chapter. Understanding the failures of those who came before us is a powerful deterrent to romanticizing and longing for the world in which they lived.[3] As Christians, we must adopt this approach. We can do this by fostering an environment in Christian educational institutions that challenges the mythology of American history with a redemptive counter-narrative that acknowledges our national sins and links these pasts to our present with a renewed call to justice. The history curriculum taught at Christian high schools and by Christian homeschooling groups is notoriously bad at this, oftentimes containing blatant errors that elevate love for nation and a desire to absolve America of its transgressive history above the work of building a kingdom-identity grounded in a culture of repentance.[4] *Some* Christian institutions of higher education are doing markedly better at this; however,

3. Howard Zinn, prolific historian and author of *A People's History of the United States*, understood this and wrote a text that has been adopted by many professors of American history in an attempt to correct the rosy, triumphalist narrative of American history that dominates secondary education in this country. See Zinn, *People's History*.

4. Lest I be accused of being against Christian schools, I should disclose that my children attend one.

by the college level, most students have a fixed perception of the American past that they are all-too-often unwilling to challenge.

There is a further challenge for the individual believer, too. The heart of this book is that Christians *must* engage the past, that it must become a part of the lived-out experience of their faith. Yet believers remain as woefully historically illiterate as the rest of the American population. This needs to change. Most Christians will never again encounter history in a substantive way after leaving college. Even those who adopt history as a sort of hobby, who become "history buffs," oftentimes find history in all the wrong places. There is a growing market for works like David McCullough's *John Adams* and other popularized accounts of the past.[5] Unfortunately, many of these works, even those written by credentialed historians, fall into the trap of nostalgia and myth-making. As informed, engaged, and educated members of the body of Christ, I would like to challenge believers to commit to begin to read academic works written by professional historians. These accounts delve into the depths of the human story, paying oftentimes painful attention to detail, and engaging with a greater analytical focus to provide a more complex, realistic view of the past that moves beyond the simple telling of a tale. This reading may be difficult and, at times, overwhelming, but there is so much at stake here. As one understands the past better, she or he can begin to live better in the present.

There is also a burden here for those of us who are professional historians. So much of our writing is given to professional considerations for our own advancement. History has become increasingly professionalized, and historical accounts are beginning to contain enough jargon to render them as indecipherable to the public as a work on advanced astrophysics. While there is a role for such in-depth studies, erudite scholarship transforms history into the province of the privileged few who possess the credentials to access it. Historians' work must be unswervingly academically rigorous, and yet, at the same time, this cannot come at the expense of cutting off accessibility to non-specialists. Historians are tasked

5. McCullough, *John Adams.*

with the sacred trust of guarding and passing along humanity's story, and we must do so in a way that makes that story accessible to all. Christian historians in particular have an obligation to democratize knowledge, to share the lesson of history, its redemptive value, and its power as a mediating narrative with our brothers and sisters in Christ. As we equip others with a better knowledge of the past, we can aid in challenging the dangers that the past can bring with it.

In addition to a woeful ignorance of the past, Christians often embrace the idol of nostalgia out of fear. The decades since the cultural revolution of the 1960s have seen increased participation in public life by women and members of minority communities, and while there is still a tremendous amount of work to be done in the quest for equality (a project that the gospel mandates we participate in), this, coupled with a changing economic landscape that has seen the large-scale loss of manufacturing jobs in the United States and the economic degradation of large swaths of the country, has engendered fear among many Americans. Many perceive themselves as standing on the edge of a cliff, about to lose the cultural and economic privileges they enjoyed throughout most of American history. These fears were seen recently on both sides of the 2016 presidential elections. The campaign rhetoric of Republican contender Donald Trump and insurgent Democrat Bernie Sanders focused on the economic plight of white workers who felt left behind in the new economy and transforming national life. In both campaigns, race and economics merged, crafting a discourse of a longing to return to a different America in which white, blue collar workers dominated the middle class.

There are two clear dangers for Christians when they embrace this form of nostalgia. The data belie the fact that this discourse is simply untrue. To be certain, there has been a profound shift away from an economy dominated by manufacturing jobs to one dominated by jobs in the service sector that has transformed life throughout much of middle America. However, median wages continue to increase for white middle class workers, and the prospects for those who claim to be left behind in the new economy are actually brighter than the pundits and armchair economists would have it. Here again we see how dangerous historical illiteracy can be. Most discussions of the economy that posit a decline for the white middle class are based on perceptions, rather than evidence, and a thorough study of the history of economic transformations in the United States over the last half-century can serve as a powerful antidote for rampant despair.

More pernicious, however, is the revived racism that this economic despondency has produced. There are growing discussions across middle America about "white plight," i.e., the perceived leaving-behind of lower-middle class and poor whites in an increasingly diversifying America. These claims have led to a pushback against civil rights agendas at the state and national level and a fear and mistrust of the Other, whether that Other is located in the black community, the Latino community, or any other minority group. As Christians, we must categorically reject this impulse, and tracing the histories of these marginalized communities into the present provides an avenue through which we can deconstruct this discourse.

Militant nostalgism is also fueled by discontent. This discontent can be rooted in the cultural discourse discussed above; much of it, however, results from the tendency for individuals to perpetually covet a situation other than the one in which they live. The long annals of Israelite history contained in the book of Numbers expose this tendency, revealing that even when God has worked great deliverance in our individual and national lives, we still long for a return to the bondage from which we came. After Moses dispatched spies to view the promised land, they brought back a favorable report of the good bounty contained therein, but stirred up fear in the camp, charging that the Israelites would in no way be able to overcome the inhabitants of the land. The people responded with a claim that echoes the nostalgism of our day:

> Then all the congregation raised a loud cry, and the people wept that night. And all the people of Israel grumbled against Moses and Aaron. The whole congregation said to them, "Would that we had died in the land of Egypt!

> Or would that we had died in the wilderness! Why is the
> Lord bringing us into this land, to fall by the sword? Our
> wives and our little ones will become a prey. Would it
> not be better for us to go back to Egypt?" And they said
> to one another, "Let us choose a leader and go back to
> Egypt." (Num 14:1-4)

Is this not the same longing that we express when we desire a return to simpler times? We wish to return to our own mythological Egypt, erasing our memories of the bondage to which we were subject in the past and the salvation that the Lord so abundantly provided for us. Had Israel but recalled its own history, acknowledged that when they cried to the Lord for deliverance in their slavery, he wrought a mighty work for their deliverance, perhaps they would have realized that the past was not what they wished it to be.

This reveals the final danger that accompanies militant nostalgism. As we long to return to the past days, when we wish for the slavery of Egypt rather than the wilderness of God, we deny our kingdom responsibilities in the present. The challenges that face our own time are daunting. Despite decades of work, there still are glaring problems of inequality in our society. The continued threat of terrorism, an increasingly unstable world, climate change, and a sluggish economy scream at us in the headlines of the daily news. We are in the wilderness of time between Christ's first advent, when the divine plan to restore the perfection of God's creation was inaugurated, and the Christ's return, when the realization of that plan will be fully actualized (more on this in the next chapter). Let us not fall into the temptation that cost the Israelites their entrance into God's rest for forty years, but rather let us acknowledge that "although salvation still lies in the future of the believer, he knows that the genuine possibilities of achievement in history are founded on the grace of God, his willingness to forgive sins and make whole by sharing a life with man."[6] Rather than seeking to return to Egypt, let us embrace the time and place to which God has called us, to create a kingdom culture in the present, and to

---

6. Lewry, *Theology of History*, 60-61.

be willing agents in the outworking of his deliverance as we live in the present working out of his reign, even as we long for its full consummation in the coming glory.

HISTORY AND THE CHALLENGE OF NEW MEDIA

Errant nostalgia is the greatest danger that Christians encounter regarding their relationship with the past and poses more than a theoretical threat to the believer. In addition to reifying racism, xenophobia, and sexism, misplaced nostalgia has engendered a growing generational conflict in American society that has crept into the church. Americans born before the 1980s often look on millennials' relationship with technology with disdain. The rise of new forms of media, including Facebook, Twitter, and Snapchat, are often met with fear and puzzlement from many within the church. Are these media destroying community? Have we transitioned our relationships from face-to-face encounters to the impersonal matrix of the online world? Do these changes threaten the body of Christ? It seems that our tendency toward nostalgia has warped our views of technology. A Christian engagement with the past can serve as a corrective to our fear of technology.

Though we must be careful to avoid constructing a point-to-point comparison between the arrival of new media in the past (for example, the printing press, radio, television, etc.) to the advent of social media (the past is a foreign country, remember!), we can extrapolate three general principles from history that can guide our engagement with such innovations. Firstly, we can learn that new media comes with new promises. The arrival of the printing press in Europe democratized learning as the price of books plummeted to levels that most could afford, increasing literacy and opening channels of information across society. In our own day, the term "Information Age" shows that the internet and, in particular, social media has facilitated the dissemination of information leading to a more equitable distribution of knowledge. Unfortunately, this has also meant that much false, misleading, and dangerous information has spread. This leads into the second principle we can learn from history about engaging the rise of social media: with new media comes new challenges. The printing press made Bibles household items, which was a positive development. However, the general availability of scripture ironically served to sever many people's relationship with the church, contributed to the rise of disunity in the body of Christ, and gave rise to a multitude of heresies. Television brought a greater awareness of current events via the medium of the evening news; however, it also came with commercials, which have greatly contributed to rampant materialism and greed in American society. The challenges of social media in our day are clear: the risk of relationships without physical contact, cyber-bullying, and disengagement with the real world are only a few. History teaches us the necessity of balancing the promise and challenge of new forms of media. Lastly, new media often ushers in social transformation. The printing press arguably contributed to the Protestant Reformation, which would have been unimaginable without the widespread availability of Bibles. The advent of television brought the horrors of segregation and Jim Crow laws to light and contributed to the rise of the Civil Rights Movement as a somber nation watched the open-casket funeral of Emmitt Till. Television also led many Americans to question the morality of the Vietnam War, the first televised war. In a similar manner, social media has drawn an otherwise apathetic public to pay attention to global affairs ranging from the refugee crisis to the ongoing struggles of black Americans. To be sure, social media also fosters a false sense of participating in campaigns for justice whereby users feel as if they accomplished something for the greater good merely by liking an image or sharing an article, but a number of social movements around the world trace their origins to social media (the 2011 Arab Spring is a good example of this). Time has yet to reveal the ways in which society will be transformed as a result of the arrival of social media; however, history cautiously permits us in the church to employ the transformational power of social media.

It is safe to conclude that our increasingly wired world will only become more so with time. The option of abstaining from new forms of media becomes less possible by the day. Yet as we as the body of Christ—in particular the older and wiser among us—fear this unknown rising tide, we must reflect again on the dangers of militant nostalgism and our fear of change and learn to adapt to the changes that whirl around us. The history of the emergence of new forms of media should encourage us that all is not lost in a rapidly changing technological landscape, even as we exercise caution about the negative impacts that media can have on our world.

CHRISTIAN TIME AS A COUNTER TO THE DANGERS OF THE PAST

In the book of Ecclesiastes, the preacher presents history as an endless cycle of humanity's vain striving in a world of unordered chaos reminiscent of Benjamin's concept of the angel of history. The preacher traces the full depths of the vanity of each human experience, including work, pleasure, love, and religion. By the end of the text, however, the narrator brings the reader back to God's redemptive purpose in the seemingly meaningless cycles of the human story: "The end of the matter; all has been heard. Fear God and keep his commandments, for this is the whole duty of man. For God will bring every deed into judgment, with every secret thing, whether good or evil" (Eccl 12:13–14). The preacher himself challenges his own paradigm of the vanity of the human story, and refuses the idolatry of nostalgism in his own day: "Say not, 'Why were the former days better than these?' For it is not from wisdom that you ask this" (Eccl 7:10). With the preacher's admonition of the wisdom of present living and rejection of nostalgism coupled with the narrator's call to fear God and keep his commandments in the present, one finds a powerful rejection of human understandings of history as a vainly repeated cycle and a corrective to the tendency toward militant nostalgism.

What is a Christian response to the secular conception of history as meaningless? How can we acknowledge the continued outpouring of God's grace across time and space, looking back to his works of goodness in the human experience and forward toward the final delivery from the cycle of time that awaits us? An answer to this dilemma can be located in the practice of the Christian liturgical year that dramatically reconceptualizes the believer's relationship with time and history.

The liturgical year radically reimagines time not as a linear cycle of vanity, as Benjamin's angel or the preacher in Ecclesiastes would have it, but rather as a divine spiral, moving into the future of God's redemption, in which the redemptive entrance of God into history—through his birth, death, and resurrection—are repeated again and again across the march of time. The Catechism of the Catholic Church declares that participation in the divine liturgy "not only recalls the events that saved us but actualizes them, makes them present,"[7] adding that through the liturgy, believers "re-read and relive the great events of salvation history in the 'today' of [the Church's] liturgy."[8] This expresses quite eloquently the purpose and nature of the practice of Christian time, whose use is being revived outside of the Catholic tradition and even in many contemporary Evangelical churches. Through re-enacting the gospel narrative in the yearly repetition of the liturgy, Christians are able to see the gospel work both *in* their lives and *through* their lives. The liturgy calls us to take the gospel, which without the liturgy often remains an abstract concept in the mind of the believer, and to live it, both through engaging believers in corporate worship and through encouraging them to walk out of the physical church building and engage the whole of the created order in light of the gospel.

Participation in the liturgy re-orients the distorted understanding of time that we possess in our rapidly globalized world, drawing us away from a so-called "flat world" and toward the fullness of God's time.[9] Our contemporary world, which above all seeks profit and ease (hence the temptation of nostalgism), has become consumed with an image of reality that preaches history as a teleological march toward progress, espoused chiefly in globaliza-

7. Catholic Church, *Catechism*, 313.
8. Catholic Church, *Catechism*, 310.
9. See Waalkes, *Fullness of Time*.

tion discourse. Standing as an alternative to this is Christian time, ever-repeating the perfection of God's soteriological purposes, yet still advancing to the day when the fullness of the kingdom will be realized.

Liturgical time allows "the church to *participate* in God's goodness,"[10] and "hints of the justice to come, hints of what God's reign looks like,"[11] challenging the idolatry of militant nostalgism. The practice of Christian time compels us to work toward reimagining our broken world and reshaping it in the image of Christ's newly inaugurated, yet not fully realized, kingdom. We are to strive against the curse of sin on our individual lives, on the collective human body, and on all of the created order. As individuals, we strive toward the righteousness of God through the indwelling of the Holy Spirit, fully aware that while we will grow in faith and right-living, we will never live up to God's standard in this life. It will only be in heaven, when God has re-ordered all our desires, that we will live, by his grace, in perfection. Similarly, we are to engage the world around us with the ideals of the kingdom. We are to work for peace, to end war, to bring justice to those to whom it has been denied, to love those who hate us, to bring peace and reconciliation to groups locked in conflict, to fight to end poverty, and to erase oppression and inequality wherever we find them. The battle will be hard, and we will never completely realize these goals on this side of eternity. However, just as the process of personal sanctification allows for the believer to grow and mature in Christ at the individual level, so, too, can we expect some victories in our battle against the curses of sin in human society as we seek to herald the kingdom of God, living in light of his appearance as man so many years ago.

Isn't this a marvelous thing? As we reimagine our relationship to time and history, we are called to worship. In turn, our worship calls us into the world. At the heart of our Christian call to engage the past, then, is worship and gospel work. History should leave us at the throne of God, bowing down in confession and adoration,

10. Waalkes, *Fullness of Time*, 21.

11. Waalkes, *Fullness of Time*, 54.

and in turn should transform our hearts with a desire to build God's kingdom in the time and place in which we live. This is the power that a Christ-centered knowledge of the past has to offer us.

CONCLUSION

History has a potent power for the believer, providing a narrative medium through which to address the question of theodicy, lessons about our own depravity, and a call to repentance for national and individual sins. But history also comes with great danger. When the past is misunderstood, when it is sifted through the sieve of nationalist myth-making, it can become to us an idol. As we look to the dangers and challenges of our own time, the temptation is strong to lust for a return to simpler times, to imagine a historical era in which the difficulties of the present fade away, and life is easy, the world is black and white.

This is a rejection of a Christian theology of history that calls us to Christ. As Christians, we must fundamentally reimagine our relationship to time and history, to challenge the temptation to militant nostalgism engendered through our historical illiteracy, our desire for power, our discontentment, and our refusal to live the ideals of the kingdom in our own time. A proper study of history, grounded in a theology that submits Christ as the Lord of time and the key that unlocks the meaning of history itself, provides a corrective to these deficits. As we explore the past, we must do so humbly, acknowledging that the allure of returning to Egypt is an illusion perpetrated by the evil one, and we must look to the kingdom of God, inaugurated in Christ, re-enacted and actualized through our worship, and lived out in our daily lives. History must become part of our faith, not just through study and reflection, but through a lived experience of the pursuit of justice grounded in the teachings of the Lord of history, the one behind the storm, the one whose kingdom purposes are being worked out throughout the human story, the one to whom all glory is owed.

7

God and the End of History

"From the beginning, the most serious and systematic attempts to write universal histories saw the central issue in history as the development of freedom. History was not a blind concentration of events, but a meaningful whole in which human ideas concerning the nature of a just political and social order developed and played themselves out. And if we are now at a point where we cannot imagine a world substantially different from our own, in which there is no apparent or obvious way in which the future will represent a fundamental improvement over our current order, then we must also take into consideration the possibility that history itself might be at an end."[1]

"The historical debate is over. The answer is free market capitalism."[2]

"And in the days of those kings the God of heaven will set up a kingdom that shall never be destroyed, nor shall the kingdom be left to another people. It shall break in pieces all these kingdoms and bring them to an end, and it shall stand forever." (Dan 2:44)

1. Fukuyama, *End of History*, 5.
2. Friedman, *Lexus*, 104.

As we established in chapter five, the past is a foreign country. Therefore, the past is a poor source for making prognostications about the future. Yet this does not stop scholars from attempting to use the past to predict the future. A most glaring example of this can be found in Francis Fukuyama's now infamous 1992 monograph, *The End of History and the Last Man*. Fukuyama, a political scientist, wrote about the collapse of the Cold War, the emergence of democracies out of the rubble of the former Soviet Union in Europe and Asia, and the emerging global positivism that characterized the world in the wake of these historic events.

Fukuyama posited that history itself was reaching its apex, the culmination of an endless quest for providing a just global society and a leveling of human relations. Fukuyama was not arguing that humanity was at its end; rather, he submitted that the process of history understood as change over time was over. Capitalism, democracy, liberal economic policies, and above all the free market had won; communism, fascism, and authoritarian governance systems had receded into the past, and humanity was set for a new course in which the ideals of the free market would reign, income inequality would be solved, and democracy would become the new norm. Gone, he argued, were the conflicts that characterized the past; the future was to be one of innovation, growth, and stability at the global level. This sentiment was repeated by many, including *New York Times* columnist Thomas Friedman in his much celebrated 2005 book *The World is Flat: A Brief History of the Twenty-First Century*, which lauded what Friedman considered to be the triumph of globalism and liberal free-market policies in much the same manner as Fukuyama.[3]

The two-and-a-half decades that have passed since the publishing of *The End of History* have categorically and forcibly proven Fukuyama wrong. The envisioned peace between the superpowers collapsed quickly as Russia and the United States entered into a revived Cold War with the former's invasion of Georgia in 2008 and the Ukraine in 2014.[4] The spread of democracy throughout the

---

3. See Friedman, *World is Flat*.

4. The Russian invasion of Ukraine in 2014 put to rest the globalist maxim

globe was halted by a new wave of authoritarian leaders—not only in the majority world but also in Europe, the supposed vanguard of democracy. The economic collapse and global recession of 2008 exposed the fault lines of liberal economic policies, and the revived populism of the 2010s challenged democratic norms throughout the globe. The fear of nuclear annihilation that governed the Cold War period gave way to the war on terror, with American military actions in Afghanistan, Iraq, and Libya, which were supposed to bring liberal democracies to those countries, ushering in new global crises that threatened the liberal order. On the domestic side, the optimism about race-relations and gender equality that defined much of the 1990s collapsed as America began to realize that perhaps we had not healed as well as we had thought from the racial injustices of our past. Far from reaching its terminus, history has come to resemble the despondent chaos beheld by Benjamin's angel more now than ever before.

This begs a question that should be at the forefront of the mind of every believer as he or she engages the past. If we are to submit Christ as the Lord and hermeneutic of history, if we are to embrace God's sovereignty over the historical process, and we are in turn to respond in worship and kingdom-building, does history itself have an end? If so, what does the Bible teach is that end? And how should this inform our God-centered engagement with the past? In this final chapter, I wish to submit that for the believer, history does have an end, though it is not the one that we would necessarily imagine. The end of history cannot be found in something human—for instance, the end of the human race or even in Christ's return to bring the human story to its conclusion—but rather the end of history can be found in the person of Christ himself. The end of history can be located at the incarnation; even as the end of time awaits Christ's second advent.

---

that no two countries that both have McDonalds have ever gone to war with one another. The idea, embraced by the likes of Fukuyama and Friedman, was that economic interdependency, the trend of the future, would bring peace.

THE ADVENT OF CHRIST AND THE END OF HISTORY

Today, when Christians talk about the end of history, it is assumed that they are referring to the second coming of Christ. Since the 1970 publication of Hal Lindsey's *The Late Great Planet Earth*, Christians, especially Evangelical Christians, have been obsessed with the end times.[5] The success of cultural works like Tim La-Haye and Jerry Jenkins's *Left Behind* series further evidences this. Lured by the temptation of escapism (in this case, an escape into a divinely ordained future rather than the desire to return to a mythological past, as discussed in the previous chapter), many Christians find themselves fantasizing about an apocalyptic end to their present troubles and a graphic display of the power of God over the forces of this world. The biblical foundations for this vision are sketchy at best.

Setting aside the potential theological flaws of the dispensationalist framework that undergirds these works (and Christ's admonition that only the Father knows the day of the Son's return), the thinking that the end of history can be located in the second advent of Christ is problematic. For the Christian, the end of history is not the second coming of Christ. Rather, to find the end, we must look to the beginning, to the foundational event of our faith. The incarnation reframes our understanding of the end of history. The decisive act of God himself entering into history by becoming a man, ushering in a kingdom bent on the destruction of the kingdoms of the world, itself conclusively enacted the end of history. History before the first advent of Christ was the unfolding of the divine plan that would lead to God's ultimate act of self-revelation. His arrival, coupled with his resurrection and ascension into glory, transforms the historical process into a master drama, leading to his return. The ultimate event in history—the humble birth of the God-man 2,000 years ago—heralded the end of history itself.

This is the meaning of Nebuchadnezzar's vision in the second chapter of Daniel. Daniel recounted the vision to the king:

5. See Lindsay, *Late Great Planet Earth*.

> You saw, O king, and behold, a great image. This image, mighty and of exceeding brightness, stood before you, and its appearance was frightening. The head of this image was of fine gold, its chest and arms of silver, its middle and thighs of bronze, its legs of iron, its feet partly of iron and partly of clay. As you looked, a stone was cut out by no human hand, and it struck the image on its feet of iron and clay, and broke them in pieces. Then the iron, the clay, the bronze, the silver, and the gold, all together were broken in pieces, and became like the chaff of the summer threshing floors; and the wind carried them away, so that not a trace of them could be found. But the stone that struck the image became a great mountain and filled the whole earth. (Dan 2:31–35)

The prophet goes on to explain that the gold, silver, bronze, iron, and clay mixed with iron signified Nebuchadnezzar's kingdom and several other great kingdoms that were to follow. While there has been no shortage of speculation over the years as to which kingdoms were specifically referenced in the prophecy, their identity is never disclosed, and conjecture distracts from the heart of the message. It is enough to say that the elements represented the kingdoms that would transverse the span of human history, and this is evidenced by Daniel's former proclamation as he introduced the vision: "He [God] changes times and seasons; he removes kings and sets up kings; he gives wisdom to the wise, and knowledge to those who have understanding" (Dan 2:21).

What is crucial to understanding the dream is not the specific identity of the elements; rather, the key lies in the identity of the stone that "was not cut out by any human hand." This stone comes and crushes all the kingdoms that came before, "so that not a trace of them could be found." This stone then goes on to become "a great mountain that filled the whole earth." What kingdom that has ever existed, or ever will exist, fits this description? Is this not the kingdom of God, inaugurated with the arrival of the king himself, which eclipses, subsumes, and destroys all the kingdoms of the world that came before and, indeed, even those that come after? Christ's coming established the divine lordship over history, destroying the endless rise and fall of empires, kingdoms, and nations that Benjamin's angel perceived in the chaos thrust before its feet. The kingdom of God, brought about as God himself entered history, *is* the end of history, the annunciation of the destruction of humanity's failed attempts at achieving glory, justice, and perfection on its own. History folds into the singularity of the incarnation. We must, therefore, locate the end of history at the point of the incarnation.

THE END OF TIME

Positing the person of Christ as the end of history does not, however, satisfactorily answer the question as to when and where the human story will reach its climax. If we are to reject Fukuyama and Friedman's globalist framework, we must posit a termination of the human story in which the full measure of its purposes will be realized. Christ's second advent, therefore, has much to bear on our understanding of history. Benjamin's angel of history was continuously falling into the future, a dismal abyss without purpose or end. Christians, however, confess that the human story has not only a logic, but a purpose, a glorious terminus in which the kingdom of God, existing already in shadow form in our present world, will transcend the temporal constraints of the human experience and will be consummated in full power. We confess that God ultimately will catch the angel of history, interrupting its fall, and place it on a new plane, one in which time folds into eternity and the chaos that characterized its seemingly never-ending fall disappears into the weight of an eternal glory (2 Cor 4:16–18).

For believers, then, while the incarnation reflects the end of history, the second coming of Christ will bring about the end of time. The difference between the two is crucial for our understanding of history. The incarnation provides the lens through which we see history. The pattern of change over time is the long story of God's restoration of his creation, the deliberate refusal of the divine to leave that which he made to its own devices as his kingdom eclipses all those of this world. As I remarked earlier, history is truly his story, the working out of his glory. Yet this story is framed within the confines of time. Unlike the divine, humanity's earthly existence is ephemeral. The process by which God brings about his salvation to the elect, works to restore his broken world, and to gather all nations and kingdoms under his rule has a limited, temporal span. The unfolding of history, acted out in the tragedy and drama of human suffering and triumph, draws us inexorably to the end of all things. The day is coming in which the rule of God through Christ will be finalized, and the book of humanity's story will be closed. On that day, we can only pray that we will be among those whose names are to be found written in the only book that matters.

Nineteenth-century pastor J. H. Newman eloquently wrote of this relationship between time, history, and Christ's advents. The incarnation, Newman submits, alters the temporal trajectory of history. Christ's entrance into the historical process directs history "not towards the end, but along it, and on the brink of it; and is at all times near that great event, which, did it run towards it, it would at once run into. Christ then is ever at our doors."[6] The picture Newman paints here is not one of history as a straight line that one day will reach an apex but rather imagines post-incarnational history as a line running parallel to the end of time itself. History after Christ has an urgency, for Christ's coming commenced its end, and, at any moment, the infinitesimal space between that which we call history and the line marking God's fixed end to the human story may close. This schematic has profound implications not just for how we view the end of history and the end of time but also challenges us to reframe our understanding of the unfolding of the human drama in relationship to God's redemptive purposes. History is firmly set within a soteriological framework, at once subsumed by the dawn of the salvation of God's people when God became man while advancing precipitously against his return and final deliverance when the divine hand will pen the conclusion to the human story.

6. Marshall, *Epistles of John*, 149.

HISTORY BETWEEN CHRIST'S ADVENTS

If history has reached its end already through the incarnation, how do we approach the human story? Certainly there is a process of change over time occurring in the liminal period between Messiah's advents. There is a string of processes and events that we could call history and that could be studied by historians, but for the Christian who seeks to explain the past, these must be read in light of the event of the incarnation and the collapse of the historical process brought about as Christ cements and ultimately claims his lordship over the nations and history itself. Paradoxically, then, history occurs after the end of history; the ultimate reality, the ultimate meaning, proceeds the working out of that meaning.

As believers, we need to frame history as the period between Christ's advents in which God's glorious plan of redemption and the outworking of Christ's rule over the nations is enacted and then fully realized. As we study history, we must acknowledge every event as being about the end of both history and time. We must recognize this, for "the history which remains is a time of tension between the 'already' of the Kingdom of God which has come in the person of Christ and the 'not yet' of a Church which awaits the advent of Christ, and prays that the Kingdom may come."[7] This tension reframes our understanding of God's sovereignty. As believers engaging the past, we must look back to the person and work of Christ, the Lord of history. We must read the longings of the human heart worked out through the historical process as the ongoing work of redemption brought about by God's entrance into history. C. S. Lewis brilliantly summarized this, offering that "all that we call human history—money, poverty, ambition, war, prostitution, classes, empires, slavery—[is] the long, terrible story of man trying to find something other than God which will make him happy."[8] Throughout history, man is looking, trying to locate his source of meaning, yet too often stubbornly refuses to find it. The angel's vain attempt to make sense of the chaos around it can

7. Lewry, *Theology of History*, 34.

8. Lewis, *Mere Christianity*, 49.

only locate its answer in the first advent of Christ. Yet we must also look ahead to the end of time. God's sovereignty is not an arbitrary display of power. His sovereignty has purpose, it has intent, and intent implies a goal. That purpose will be fulfilled when time gives way to eternity.

This requires that we rethink our understanding of the kingdom of God. In the early twentieth century, modernist Christianity assumed that the kingdom would be achieved on earth, as advances in technology and governance brought about a just society, a literal fulfillment of Christ's thousand year reign (Rev 20:1–3). Dispensationalists, whose framework dominates many popular Christian understandings of the end times, posit that the kingdom is coming when Christ returns. Neither of these is correct, yet neither is completely wrong, either. The kingdom exists, for the king has come. Those who beheld Christ during his earthly ministry gazed upon the kingdom (Luke 7:21). The history of the church, drawn together by Christ from all nations, tribes, and languages, is the beginning of his reign and the outworking of his soteriological purposes. Yet the kingdom is not yet fully actualized. The kingdom that brings about the end of history is still working itself out in a temporal process, yet that process draws ever closer to its terminus, to the time in which Christ's reign will be complete, the moment at which time itself will vanish. Thus we live in a kingdom that is present, yet a kingdom that also has not yet come.

This framework demonstrates another way in which the study of the past is edifying for the believer. In contemporary Christian parlance, the term "gospel" has been taken on a strictly soteriological meaning. When most Christians speak of "spreading the gospel," they employ the moniker to mean the good news that Christ's sacrificial death was offered as a propitiation to stay God's wrath at sin. Yet, scripturally speaking, this is only a portion of the good news that Christ had to offer. The fullest meaning of the word as it is revealed in the New Testament is that the arrival of the kingdom of God in the person of Christ is itself the gospel. Since as we witness history unfold we behold the growing kingdom of God, studying the past should reveal to us the gospel. Our study of history, then, should be an extension of our study of the good news of Christ as we have the privilege of watching his kingdom envelop and ultimately crush all the false kingdoms of this world.

THE KINGDOM OF GOD AND THE STUDY OF THE PAST

Embracing the paradoxical nature of God's already established yet not fully actualized kingdom present in the era between Christ's advents gives us a sense of our own responsibility as agents in the hand of an all-sovereign God, allows us to see the dynamics of the kingdom in our own time, and calls us to hope. Framing history as existing between the end of history—actualized by the incarnation and the end of time at Christ's return—should lead us to assess our responsibilities in the time and space in which we live. As Lewis argued, so much of the human experience is the story of mankind's attempts to fill its longings with something less than divine, to try to solve the predicament of our sin by ourselves. This is a fruitless endeavor. Yet if the kingdom is now present with us, even if not yet fully realized, we as Christians have an alternate paradigm for seeking temporal progress in human society. Thinkers like Fukuyama and Friedman posit the goal of history as the creation of a just, equitable society that is profitable for all. As Christians, we are working toward this very same goal. Justice is an ideal of the kingdom, and well-formed theology of the already-not-yet nature of the kingdom of God calls us to live out kingdom ideals in the here-and-now, knowing that (contrary to Fukuyama and Friedman), while this "goal of human history may never be achieved, the unity of mankind may never become a complete reality, and the day on which 'the Eternal shall be King over the earth' may require a culminating act of divine grace and love . . . man's own responsibility never ceases, for his opportunity to bring the goal to closer realization is never lost."[9] Our responsibility as ambassadors of the king of history is to work toward realizing the fullness of

9. Berkovits, *God, Man, and History*, 156–57.

his reign, to embrace the principles he taught us, and to attempt to recreate, to the greatest extent possible, the glorious reality into which he is calling us, even as we acknowledge that we will be unable to attain that reality in the time between his advents.

This draws us back to the tension between divine sovereignty and human agency that we first encountered in the second chapter. God is sovereign over all of human history, and he alone is the agent driving the historical process. Yet this does not absolve us of any responsibility. As Christians, we bear the name of Christ, not only in our title as a religious community, but in our lives, too. By his grace and election, we are his ambassadors, the bureaucrats in his kingdom who are called to enact the divine policy. The church, those whom God has chosen to be his kingdom in the temporal span of history, must reflect the glories of the king. Yet at the end of the day, we must submit that our agency is subsumed under the divine agency, humbling confessing that "we are unworthy servants, we have only done what was our duty" (Luke 17:10b).

Reading history through the lens of the kingdom of God also invites us to acknowledge the dynamics of the kingdom in the present. Looking to the end of time gives us the grace of seeing God's good nature in our own time: "A theology of history can talk about the future and even about the end of history if it is recognized that the eschatological statements are founded on the future-directed, promise-character of our present knowledge of Christ, and that the end of history, in the sense of its conclusion, is present to us mysteriously with the appreciation that faith brings of what history is aiming at. Although the fulfilment cannot be foreseen in all its novelty, the promise here and now is a solid experience of the future."[10] God's good promises concerning the actualization of his kingdom that is already present with us should provide us with a sense of rest. If God is sovereign, and that sovereignty is working toward a future purpose, we can trust God in the moment. As the world swirls about us, the rubbish heap of history piles at our feet, and we cannot make sense of it all, we can humbly submit to the knowledge that history has an aim, that the divine purpose is

10. Lewry, *Theology of History*, 86.

unfolding before us, and the kingdom continues its advance as we await the return of the king. This should lead us to contentment even in the worst of times, though that is perhaps easier said than done. But if we live our lives in full awareness of the liminal epoch in which find ourselves, through the Spirit's leading, we can take comfort. Christ came in fulfillment of the promises God made for the deliverance of his creation from the beginning and can be trusted to fulfill all of his good purposes toward us even as time draws to a close (Gen 3:15).

This leads us into the final way in which a realized-eschatological framing of history strengthens our faith. As we look to time's end, to the final realization of the purposes of God, we can draw hope. As we wring our hands at the world around us, we recognize that "the uncertainty of the future into which history is taking us might be unbearable unless some beacon up ahead lights our way and guides us through the fog toward some vision of fulfillment."[11] Without the sure knowledge that time will end, that there will be a limit to the suffering that marks our present existence, we would be right to despair. Yet as we locate our lives in the already-not-yet of the kingdom of God, "the substance of biblical faith allows us to say, at the very least, the following: without a trust in the promise of a meaningful and unimaginably fulfilling future, the move into history would be intolerable. History without promise is unbearable."[12] We have the sure promise of God's purpose, and we can rejoice in the knowledge that the pains of the human story will come to an end.

When we skim the pages of the human story, and we read the darkest of tales, the Holocaust, the Transatlantic Slave Trade, Indian removal, and so many others, it is tempting to despair, to lose hope, and to question the sovereignty of God. But we cannot fully grasp God's purpose unfolding in our bounded temporal existence. For God, a day is as a thousand years and a thousand years a day (2 Pet 3:8), for the divine exists out of the scope of time and history (though in Christ he entered both). The day is

11. Haught, *Revelation*, 35.

12. Haught, *Revelation*, 36.

coming when this evil will be destroyed, when the curse of sin will be ultimately and completely abolished, when the perpetrators of injustice will be brought to justice, and the sufferers will be liberated. The end of time and the coming ultimate lordship of Christ should cause us to rejoice, even if we cannot understand the divine purpose in the here and now. The day is ever drawing even nearer in which that purpose will reach its fruition, and though we will most likely still not comprehend it then, we should rejoice now in that fact. Despair not as you study history, but rejoice, for the story shall end, the era of humanity's wicked inclinations will be brought to a close, and the God of justice shall reign supreme.

CONCLUSION

This schema of history and time may seem perplexing. By situating the end of history at the incarnation, we confess that history ended before it even truly began. Yet the human experience continues to unfold over the span of time, leading us to the paradox that history continues even after it has ended. And what a happy paradox this is! Many are the times in which I find myself engrossed in a good tale, unable to put a book down, yet find myself fearful that the story will not end as I wish. I stay up late into the night, poring over each page as fast as I can, seeking to find the end, to know that all will work out as I wish. Too often that hope is dashed by a surprise ending, or a tale whose ending is not truly an end at all. What great disappointment this leaves me with! In these instances, I often write my own ending in my mind, seeking to fill in the void left by what I perceive to be an author's betrayal.

Yet thanks be to God, the divine author has not betrayed us! The human story continues to unfold around us, as it has done since the birth of Messiah. It is perplexing and intriguing, full of drama, tragedy, comedy, and irony. It is the greatest of tales, yet so often it is full of heartache and unbearable tragedy. As we look at the world around us, the great story of our fallen race, we often fall into the same despair that I do when reading a good book. How will the story end? Who will win in the end? Will all the drama be resolved? Will any of this we are experiencing ever really matter?

The good news with the human story is that the end has been given to us before the beginning. We can anchor our hope throughout the ups and downs, through each sordid turn in the tale, through tragedy and triumph, in the firm knowledge that our tale's hero has already won the battle. The author of the human drama has solved every twist and turn of his story by entering into that story himself as the hero, and wrought his great deliverance even before the first chapter. And what a hope that is! We need not fret, need not worry, as we look to the seeming tragedy of our existence, for the calamity has already been erased: the kingdom is here! Our task now is to act out the play that God has written, and as we experience the darker scenes, to rejoice that the time is rapidly approaching in which the curtains will close, the lights will raise, and God will bring us to an everlasting celebration in which we will revel in his triumph for all eternity.

Conclusion

"The night Effia Otcher was born into the musky heat of Fanteland, a fire raged through the woods just outside her father's compound. It moved quickly, tearing a path for days. It lived off the air; it slept in caves and hid in trees; it burned, up and through, unconcerned with what wreckage it left behind, until it reached an Asante village. There it disappeared, becoming one with the night. Effia's father. . .knew then that the memory of the fire that burned, then fled, would haunt him, his children, and his children's children for as long as the line continued."[1]

"Remember the days of old; consider the years of many generations; ask your father, and he will show you, your elders, and they will tell you." (Deut 32:7)

"For inquire, please, of bygone ages, and consider what the fathers have searched out. For we are but of yesterday and know nothing, for our days on earth are a shadow." (Job 8:8–9)

HOMEGOING, THE OUTSTANDING FIRST novel by author Yaa Gyasi, begins with a fire that consumes a seventeenth-century family's

1. Gyasi, *Homegoing*, 3. Gyasi's novel, which involved seven years of rigorous historical research to write, is an excellent place to begin if one is interested in wrestling with the ways in which the past informs the present. In particular, her work reveals in narrative form the deep ways in which America's history with slavery and segregation have impacted out contemporary society.

world in what is present-day Ghana. The novel traces two lines of the family through the next three centuries; one, whose descendants were sold into slavery in the Americas, and the other, who remained behind in Ghana. For the branch of the family in America, water becomes a haunting motif, a constant echo of the horrors of the transatlantic voyage that first thrust them upon the shores of a new continent. For those who remained in Ghana, the fire that chased Effia haunted her ancestors, returning every generation to remind the family of its troubled past. Though history did not repeat itself for the characters in the novel, it also did not die for them. The past was always present, for good or for ill, and a necessary component of their day-to-day lives.

History functions in much the same manner, for that which is past is actually present with us. It informs the world in which we live and has charted the very path that we are presently on. Like the angel of history, we face the past as we are blown into the future. We wish, as did the angel, to close our wings, to shield ourselves from the storm that besets us, yet we have not the power to do so. We share with the preacher in Ecclesiastes a knowledge that life itself is but a vapor. We, like the characters in Gyasi's novel, long for the memory of the time that came before us, a time in which there was innocence and hope. But that world has burned away. Our lives ache for meaning, for a lasting impact. We cry for eternity. We scramble to and fro to make our own meaning, to try to carve a place for ourselves within the broader fabric of the human story, yet all our efforts seem to come up short. We, too, will be forgotten as the long march of time leaves us in the heap of rubbish hurled at the angel as it plods along.

What is the cure for the hopelessness that has come to characterize so many lives in our age? Is there any way to break this seemingly unending cycle, to stop the storm that blows from Paradise and propels us into the abyss of the future? As Christians, we are not condemned to this fate. Yet it is easy to find ourselves trapped in the same mentality. The world around us flings false gods before our face, idols meant to dull our sense of meaninglessness in an ever changing world. We lose our sense of place as part of the unfolding divine drama as we try to insert ourselves as the authors of our own story.

As we have covered in the last seven chapters, a Christ-centered approach to history can draw us out of this hopeless quest. History allows us to question God when he seems to be invisible, lays bare our depravity, calls us to repent, challenges our discontent in the present, and opens our eyes to the future. History leads us to a sense of place in the world, to an understanding of ourselves as part of a larger plan, a story that does not end when we depart the scene. History draws us to hope when all else seems lost, for history points us back to the one who has overcome the seemingly unordered chaos that besets our lives.

HISTORY AND THE BELIEVER

We have reached the end—or, perhaps more accurately, an end. History itself found its end in the coming of the Lord of history, yet the historical process still works out until his return. Our own lives, our personal histories, will soon come to a close, and the memory of our small part in the grand human narrative will pass. The meaning we poured into our lives will be gone. Nations and empires fall around us, still under the sovereignty of the divine. Our nations, our faith communities, and our families will join the long rolls of those who have gone before us as history unfolds into eternity.

Is it all meaningless then? Life is but passing wind. We are born, and before we know it, our story has been written, only to be forgotten. Yet herein is our reason to rejoice. Though we may be tempted to despair, to join our lot with the angel of history as it is blown off the annals of time, to stare in confusion at the mess of our own existence, at the ephemeral nature of the kingdoms we have built around us, we need not mourn. The author of our story has not left us to despair, but has given us hope, for this is not truly our story, but his. We have been brought into the tale at the moment of his design to fulfill our part in the unfolding plot, and when our act is over, he gives us our exit. But we are more than just characters for our author. While the brief span of our lives must unfold in the context of the divine drama that we know as history, we were made for eternity, for fellowship, and the day will soon dawn in which we will spend eternity recounting the tales of our divine author, celebrating his victory over the storm mistaken for progress that blows us into the future.

The past seven chapters have provided a means through which we can anticipate that celebration, a taste of the eternal worship service to come when we stand before the Lord of history and recount his many great deeds. As we form our faith historically and as we engage the past christologically, we are given a glimpse of the greatness that is to come.

In the first chapter, we saw the fruitlessness of trying to make sense of the past without God. Humanity has striven in vain to assert its own mastery over the historical process, and has always fallen short. The paradigm of postmodernism that now dominates historical inquiry posits that humanity makes its own meaning, that truth is a product of history, and that humanity possesses the power to create facts. To be sure, as we discussed, humanity has frequently tried to produce its own truths. The discourse of race that has so marred our chapter of the human story is an example of this. But history devoid of immutable fact is hollow, for it can never be reconciled to the existence of the divine. Our assertion of truth is grounded in the fact that truth stems not from discourse, nor from human invention, but can be solely located in the person of Christ, the Lord of history.

Humanity cannot manufacture its own history. Try as it might, the angel of history cannot make sense of the debris pilling up at its feet nor can it stop the storm that blows it toward a frightening, unknown future. It cannot even sense an end to its tumbling. When we remove the possibility of *a priori* truth, as postmodernism does, we find ourselves groping about in the dark, trying to feel our way through a valley of shadows with no sense of the world around us. Truth is necessary to make sense of the human experience. Truth grounds us in the corporeal, lends reality to the suffering that we experience in this world, and provides the means through which we can make sense of the swirl around us that is history. In doing so, truth provides us with a blessed hope of the coming close of the historical drama as history and time fade into the full glory of the kingdom of God.

This then led us in the second chapter to posit an alternative paradigm in which truth not only exists independent of human construction, but has been revealed to us in the historical drama as God himself entered into human history. If we are to reject postmodernism's claim that truth is subjective, that facts are mere fancies of our imaginative attempts to assert our own power and position in the world, we must embrace a God of truth. What is more, we must reject the notion that history is meaningless, advanced by a storm mistaken for progress. God himself is the author of history, and he retains absolute sovereignty over every facet of the human experience. We must be willing to let go of our selfish need to assert our own agency and rejoice in this divine sovereignty.

Isn't this a wonderful thought? We need not fear the storm about us, the debris behind us, or the chaos piling at our feet. If God is the author of history, then this is already sorted out. The darkest chapters of the human story fold under the sovereign hand of the divine. The divine story, unfolding in the temporal span of human history, has a beginning, it has a logic, and—most fortunate for us—it has a clear end. That end can be located in the kingdom of God revealed through the coming of Christ and soon to be consummated at his return. Though we cannot understand every chapter of the human story, even as we question God's goodness in faith, we can rest assured that all is drawing toward a glorious reality to come, and that no one, whether king, emperor, or our own fallen selves, can subvert.

Yet there are still areas of glaring and obvious doubt, as we covered in the third chapter. If God is sovereign, and if he is likewise good, why do bad things happen? Why does it appear as if the worst forms of evil are given reign throughout the long, sad story of humanity? As we are not the authors of the human story, we can never fully appreciate the nuance of the divine drama as it plays out around us. Yet God has given us history as a narrative medium through which we can mediate these questions, even if we are left without a conclusive answer. History provides us with a playing field in which we can exercise our doubts, a space where we may inquire of the divine in a manner that philosophizing alone could never accomplish. As we question the ways of the author of the human story, we are drawn back to his goodness, even if the only answer we are left with is to confess his sovereignty against our frailty.

A Christian approach to history provides us an avenue through which we can elevate the experiences of those who have suffered the most in the human drama. Christ's call that we attend the needs of "the least of these" (Matt 25:40) rings out as we listen to the marginalized voices from the past. History gives those voices strength, allowing them to articulate their grievances, and provides an avenue of redress for those who have been silenced in our own society. History, then, becomes a powerful tool for fostering a kingdom-centered pursuit of justice within our own times.

As we processed in the fourth chapter, history also functions as our teacher, yet not in the way we often wish it to be. While it is tempting to look to the past and to read it into the circumstances of our own times, history does not work in this way. It is not enough to look at the lives of those who came before us and to claim, self-righteously, that we will not commit the same evils that they have. Had we been born in a different context, we might have found ourselves caught up in the very same sins as our forefathers and foremothers. Through appropriating history as a tutor that prevents us from repeating its mistakes, we neglect to acknowledge the evils present with us in the time in which we live. No amount of historical proficiency will guard us against these evils; rather, we must humbly question the dominate forces in the society around us and rise to face the dark evil present among us.

Our misguided attempts to absolve ourselves of the sins of the past by casting ourselves in the role of the hero, or rescuer, fall apart as we realize that we are, in fact, the villain. History reveals to us the depths of our own depravity, drawing us back to the goodness of the one who entered into history to rid our world of the evils that we allow to enter it. Studying the past, then, becomes a profitable exercise for Christians as history becomes the mirror that reflects back the image of the worst parts of our nature. We must in turn learn to accept what we see and to seek cleansing and a changed heart as we turn in humble submission to the Lord of history.

We must not remain, however, before the mirror to behold our inadequacy and cry for mercy but rather, as outlined in the fifth chapter, we must openly confess and repent from the sins committed by those who have gone before us. As the Psalmist confessed, we must acknowledge that we have sinned with our fathers and our mothers, and we share in their guilt. There is a powerful recalcitrance to admit to guilt at the corporate level, especially when the honor of our nation or our faith is at stake, but this is precisely what a Christ-centered approach to history demands of us.

We must challenge the triumphalist narratives of history that form the bedrock of our national and ecclesial narratives and openly acknowledge the dark chapters of our history. We must remake or, at the very least, reconceptualize historical spaces, understanding that, against all the hope espoused by our national ideals, there is a sordid and difficult background that remains present with us. As we turn redemptively to the past, we must challenge the historical legacies of injustice, such as racism, that still linger with us. A Christ-formed study of the past should lead us to reallocate our resources in the present toward our brothers and sisters who have faced historical oppression, the legacies of which still haunt us. We must produce concrete results to right historic wrongs if history is to have any meaning for us today.

But as much as the past has to offer for our edification, a fraudulent understanding of history can lead to a misguided desire to return to the past, as we saw in the sixth chapter. We must be wary of the siren-call of escapism, the desire to return to a mythological past in which the concerns of the present are washed away. We like to imagine ourselves in the world of Mayberry, a land in which the forces that divide us—racism, classism, sexism, homophobia,

Bibliography

Balthasar, Hans Urs Von. *A Theology of History*. San Francisco: Ignatius, 1963.

Barthes, Roland. *Mythologies*. Translated by Annette Lavers. New York: Hill and Wang, 1972.

Bhabha, Homi K. *The Location of Culture*. London: Routledge, 1994.

Benjamin, Walter. *Theses on the Philosophy of History*. Translated by Harry Zohn. New York: Schocken, 1969.

Berkovits, Eliezer. *God, Man, and History*. Jerusalem: Shalem, 2004.

Boice, James Montgomery. *God and History*. Leicester, UK: Intervarsity, 1981.

Brown, Callum. *Postmodernism for Historians*. New York: Routledge, 2004.

Browning, Christopher R. *Ordinary Men: Reserve Police Battalion 101 and the Final Solution in Poland*. New York: Harper, 1992.

Catholic Church. *Catechism of the Catholic Church: Revised in Accordance with the Official Latin Text Promulgated by Pope John Paul II*. 2nd ed. New York: Doubleday, 1995.

Conyers, A. J. *God, Hope, and History: Jürgen Moltmann and the Christian Concept of History*. Macon, GA: Mercer University Press, 1988.

Foucault, Michel. *The History of Sexuality*. New York: Vintage, 1990.

Friedman, Thomas. *The Lexus and the Olive Tree*. New York: Picador, 2012.

———. *The World is Flat: A Brief History of the Twenty-First Century*. New York: FSG, 2005.

Fukuyama, Francis. *The End of History and the Last Man*. New York: Free Press, 1992.

Goldhagen, Daniel Jonah. *Hitler's Willing Executioners: Ordinary Germans and the Holocaust*. New York: Vintage, 1997.

Guldi, Jo, and David Armitage. *The History Manifesto*. Cambridge: Cambridge University Press, 2014.

Gyasi, Yaa. *Homegoing*. New York: Knopf, 2016.

Hartley, L. P. *The Go-Between*. London: Penguin, 1953.

Haught, John F. *The Revelation of God in History*. Wilmington, DE: Michael Clazier, 1988.

"History and Narrative." *Musalaha*. 20 February 2017. http://www.musalaha.org/articles/2017/2/20/history-and-narrative.

Jones, Adam. *Genocide: A Comprehensive Introduction*. New York: Routledge, 2006.

Kidner, Derek. *The Message of Ecclesiastes.* Leicester, UK: Intervarsity, 1976.

Lewis, C. S. *Mere Christianity.* New York: HarperOne, 1952.

Lewry, Osmund. *The Theology of History.* Notre Dame, IN: Fides, 1969.

Lindsay, Hal. *The Late Great Planet Earth.* Grand Rapids, MI, 1970.

Lockner, Louis P. *What about Germany?* New York: Dodd, Mead & Co., 1942.

Marshall, I. H. *The Epistles of John.* Grand Rapids, MI: Eerdmans, 1978.

McCullough, David. *John Adams.* New York: Simon & Schuster, 2001.

Moltmann, Jürgen. *History and the Triune God: Contributions to Trinitarian Theology.* New York: Crossroad, 1992.

Ortlund, Raymond C. *Isaiah: God Saves Sinners.* Wheaton, IL: Crossway, 2005.

Ricketts, Paul. "Move in Our Midst." *Friends Journal.* http://www.friendsjournal.org/move-in-our-midst.

Santayana, George. *The Life of Reason, or, The Phases of Human Progress.* New York: Scribner, 1905.

Scott, Joan Wallach. *Gender and the Politics of History.* New York: Columbia University Press, 1988.

Smuts, Adriaan. "Amnesty Application." *Truth and Reconciliation Commission.* 12 August 1996. Transcript. http://www.justice.gov.za/trc/amntrans%5Cdurban/smuts.htm.

Snyder, Timothy. *Black Earth: The Holocaust as History and Warning.* New York: Tim Duggan, 2015.

Spurgeon, C. H. *The Treasury of David: An Original Exposition of the Book of Psalms.* Peabody, MA: Hendrickson.

Stump, Eleonore. *Wandering in Darkness: Narrative and the Problem of Suffering.* Oxford: Oxford University Press, 2010.

Tolkien, J. R. R. *The Lord of the Rings: The Fellowship of the Ring.* New York: DelRey, 2012.

Tutu, Desmond, and Mpho Tutu. *The Book of Forgiving: The Fourfold Path for Healing Ourselves and Our World.* San Francisco: Harper One, 2014.

Waalkes, Scott. *The Fullness of Time in a Flat World: Globalization and the Liturgical Year.* Eugene, OR: Cascade, 2010.

White, Hayden. *Metahistory: The Historical Imagination in Nineteenth Century Europe.* Baltimore: Johns Hopkins University Press, 1973.

Zinn, Howard. *A People's History of the United States.* New York: Harper and Row, 1980.

characters for our author. While the brief span of our lives must unfold in the context of the divine drama that we know as history, we were made for eternity, for fellowship, and the day will soon dawn in which we will spend eternity recounting the tales of our divine author, celebrating his victory over the storm mistaken for progress that blows us into the future.

The past seven chapters have provided a means through which we can anticipate that celebration, a taste of the eternal worship service to come when we stand before the Lord of history and recount his many great deeds. As we form our faith historically and as we engage the past christologically, we are given a glimpse of the greatness that is to come.

In the first chapter, we saw the fruitlessness of trying to make sense of the past without God. Humanity has striven in vain to assert its own mastery over the historical process, and has always fallen short. The paradigm of postmodernism that now dominates historical inquiry posits that humanity makes its own meaning, that truth is a product of history, and that humanity possesses the power to create facts. To be sure, as we discussed, humanity has frequently tried to produce its own truths. The discourse of race that has so marred our chapter of the human story is an example of this. But history devoid of immutable fact is hollow, for it can never be reconciled to the existence of the divine. Our assertion of truth is grounded in the fact that truth stems not from discourse, nor from human invention, but can be solely located in the person of Christ, the Lord of history.

Humanity cannot manufacture its own history. Try as it might, the angel of history cannot make sense of the debris piling up at its feet nor can it stop the storm that blows it toward a frightening, unknown future. It cannot even sense an end to its tumbling. When we remove the possibility of *a priori* truth, as postmodernism does, we find ourselves groping about in the dark, trying to feel our way through a valley of shadows with no sense of the world around us. Truth is necessary to make sense of the human experience. Truth grounds us in the corporeal, lends reality to the suffering that we experience in this world, and provides the means through which we can make sense of the swirl around us that is history. In doing so, truth provides us with a blessed hope of the coming close of the historical drama as history and time fade into the full glory of the kingdom of God.

This then led us in the second chapter to posit an alternative paradigm in which truth not only exists independent of human construction, but has been revealed to us in the historical drama as God himself entered into human history. If we are to reject postmodernism's claim that truth is subjective, that facts are mere fancies of our imaginative attempts to assert our own power and position in the world, we must embrace a God of truth. What is more, we must reject the notion that history is meaningless, advanced by a storm mistaken for progress. God himself is the author of history, and he retains absolute sovereignty over every facet of the human experience. We must be willing to let go of our selfish need to assert our own agency and rejoice in this divine sovereignty.

Isn't this a wonderful thought? We need not fear the storm about us, the debris behind us, or the chaos piling at our feet. If God is the author of history, then this is already sorted out. The darkest chapters of the human story fold under the sovereign hand of the divine. The divine story, unfolding in the temporal span of human history, has a beginning, it has a logic, and—most fortunate for us—it has a clear end. That end can be located in the kingdom of God revealed through the coming of Christ and soon to be consummated at his return. Though we cannot understand every chapter of the human story, even as we question God's goodness in faith, we can rest assured that all is drawing toward a glorious reality to come, and that no one, whether king, emperor, or our own fallen selves, can subvert.

Yet there are still areas of glaring and obvious doubt, as we covered in the third chapter. If God is sovereign, and if he is likewise good, why do bad things happen? Why does it appear as if the worst forms of evil are given reign throughout the long, sad story of humanity? As we are not the authors of the human story, we can never fully appreciate the nuance of the divine drama as it plays out around us. Yet God has given us history as a narrative medium through which we can mediate these questions, even if we are left without a conclusive answer. History provides us with a playing field in which we can exercise our doubts, a space where we may inquire of the divine in a manner that philosophizing alone could never accomplish. As we question the ways of the author of the human story, we are drawn back to his goodness, even if the only answer we are left with is to confess his sovereignty against our frailty.

A Christian approach to history provides us an avenue through which we can elevate the experiences of those who have suffered the most in the human drama. Christ's call that we attend the needs of "the least of these" (Matt 25:40) rings out as we listen to the marginalized voices from the past. History gives those voices strength, allowing them to articulate their grievances, and provides an avenue of redress for those who have been silenced in our own society. History, then, becomes a powerful tool for fostering a kingdom-centered pursuit of justice within our own times.

As we processed in the fourth chapter, history also functions as our teacher, yet not in the way we often wish it to be. While it is tempting to look to the past and to read it into the circumstances of our own times, history does not work in this way. It is not enough to look at the lives of those who came before us and to claim, self-righteously, that we will not commit the same evils that they have. Had we been born in a different context, we might have found ourselves caught up in the very same sins as our forefathers and foremothers. Through appropriating history as a tutor that prevents us from repeating its mistakes, we neglect to acknowledge the evils present with us in the time in which we live. No amount of historical proficiency will guard us against these evils; rather, we must humbly question the dominate forces in the society around us and rise to face the dark evil present among us.

Our misguided attempts to absolve ourselves of the sins of the past by casting ourselves in the role of the hero, or rescuer, fall apart as we realize that we are, in fact, the villain. History reveals to us the depths of our own depravity, drawing us back to the goodness of the one who entered into history to rid our world of the evils that we allow to enter it. Studying the past, then, becomes a profitable exercise for Christians as history becomes the mirror that reflects back the image of the worst parts of our nature. We must in turn learn to accept what we see and to seek cleansing and a changed heart as we turn in humble submission to the Lord of history.

We must not remain, however, before the mirror to behold our inadequacy and cry for mercy but rather, as outlined in the fifth chapter, we must openly confess and repent from the sins committed by those who have gone before us. As the Psalmist confessed, we must acknowledge that we have sinned with our fathers and our mothers, and we share in their guilt. There is a powerful recalcitrance to admit to guilt at the corporate level, especially when the honor of our nation or our faith is at stake, but this is precisely what a Christ-centered approach to history demands of us.

We must challenge the triumphalist narratives of history that form the bedrock of our national and ecclesial narratives and openly acknowledge the dark chapters of our history. We must remake or, at the very least, reconceptualize historical spaces, understanding that, against all the hope espoused by our national ideals, there is a sordid and difficult background that remains present with us. As we turn redemptively to the past, we must challenge the historical legacies of injustice, such as racism, that still linger with us. A Christ-formed study of the past should lead us to reallocate our resources in the present toward our brothers and sisters who have faced historical oppression, the legacies of which still haunt us. We must produce concrete results to right historic wrongs if history is to have any meaning for us today.

But as much as the past has to offer for our edification, a fraudulent understanding of history can lead to a misguided desire to return to the past, as we saw in the sixth chapter. We must be wary of the siren-call of escapism, the desire to return to a mythological past in which the concerns of the present are washed away. We like to imagine ourselves in the world of Mayberry, a land in which the forces that divide us—racism, classism, sexism, homophobia, religious tribalism, economic inequality—are whitewashed out of the picture. We should never set the past up as an idol but rather learn to live within the chapter of the human story in which God has written us. We must address the problems of our own time while acknowledging the difficulties of the past. This challenge to the pervasive nostalgia that has eclipsed our culture forces us to rethink our relationship to emerging technologies in the present. Rather than fearing the world about us with its ever changing information landscape, we must learn to embrace change, to find peace in our ever-changing society, even as we acknowledge the challenges that new media and other forces that dominate our world can bring.

We can counter the siren call of misplaced nostalgia by returning to the practice of Christian time. The liturgical year grounds us in the present while recounting the glories of the sacred past. The actualizing of grace brought about through the liturgy allows us to simultaneously exist as historical beings while calling us to live in the present. This belies that a Christian call to engage the past must be accompanied by a call to worship, to recounting the glorious triumph of Christ over the forces of history, and to anticipate our coming redemption.

The final chapter brought home the ways in which history can point us toward this hope of salvation to come. The divine author has written the end of the story by his own entrance into the tale. The coming of Christ's kingdom that began with his becoming man heralds the end of history itself. The kingdom of God in Christ eclipses all that came before, all that has come since, and all that is yet to come, through the temporal span of human existence. We then need to read history in light of its already accomplished end, and doing so should point us back toward our savior.

Yet we must not be content to stop here, for while we can locate the end of history at the moment of the incarnation, we still long to see the day in which the angel of history's tragic lurching toward the future is brought to a sudden halt. Time, like history, must have an end, and as we read the pages of the past, we should be drawn toward the hope of that end. As we look about us and see the hopelessness of the human condition, as we envision humanity on a seemingly endless downward trajectory, we confess that this suffering will not go on forever. As historical beings, our existence is bookended by the end of history brought about by the incarnation and the end of time marked by Christ's return. This "already-not yet" approach to history commands us to live out the kingdom during our own part of the divine story while forcing us to anticipate the closing of the book. In this way, history leaves us in the perfect tension of the kingdom of God that is present among us, yet is not realized in its full power.

CONCLUSION

The study of the past is a profitable endeavor for the believer, transforming the way in which we interact with the world around us, sanctifying us, and leading us to a better understanding of our Lord. Though many may find the subject to be dull, uninteresting, and pointless, history must become a meaningful force in the life of Christian. A Christ-formed approach to history has the power to transform our faith. Tapping into that power should become a regular part of every Christian's walk. The process may be difficult, but the time spent will be well worth it. So I encourage you now, as you prepare to close this book, to take into consideration the ways in which history can become a part of your daily life. Take the time and effort to learn history, not as an intellectual exercise, but as a part of your faith journey. It may be helpful to begin with subjects that interest you, but make the commitment to dive into the human story. Engage the past, transform your present, and hope for that which is yet to come. Get to know the author of the human drama better as you study, and may God reward you richly as you read the masterful tale he has written, a story that points back to him.

And so, as we reach the end of this book, yet not the end of the human story itself, we can simply join with the hymnist in worship, praying "And so let thy glory Almighty impart; through Christ in his story, thy Christ to the heart."

Bibliography

Balthasar, Hans Urs Von. *A Theology of History*. San Francisco: Ignatius, 1963.

Barthes, Roland. *Mythologies*. Translated by Annette Lavers. New York: Hill and Wang, 1972.

Bhabha, Homi K. *The Location of Culture*. London: Routledge, 1994.

Benjamin, Walter. *Theses on the Philosophy of History*. Translated by Harry Zohn. New York: Schocken, 1969.

Berkovits, Eliezer. *God, Man, and History*. Jerusalem: Shalem, 2004.

Boice, James Montgomery. *God and History*. Leicester, UK: Intervarsity, 1981.

Brown, Callum. *Postmodernism for Historians*. New York: Routledge, 2004.

Browning, Christopher R. *Ordinary Men: Reserve Police Battalion 101 and the Final Solution in Poland*. New York: Harper, 1992.

Catholic Church. *Catechism of the Catholic Church: Revised in Accordance with the Official Latin Text Promulgated by Pope John Paul II*. 2nd ed. New York: Doubleday, 1995.

Conyers, A. J. *God, Hope, and History: Jürgen Moltmann and the Christian Concept of History*. Macon, GA: Mercer University Press, 1988.

Foucault, Michel. *The History of Sexuality*. New York: Vintage, 1990.

Friedman, Thomas. *The Lexus and the Olive Tree*. New York: Picador, 2012.

———. *The World is Flat: A Brief History of the Twenty-First Century*. New York: FSG, 2005.

Fukuyama, Francis. *The End of History and the Last Man*. New York: Free Press, 1992.

Goldhagen, Daniel Jonah. *Hitler's Willing Executioners: Ordinary Germans and the Holocaust*. New York: Vintage, 1997.

Guldi, Jo, and David Armitage. *The History Manifesto*. Cambridge: Cambridge University Press, 2014.

Gyasi, Yaa. *Homegoing*. New York: Knopf, 2016.

Hartley, L. P. *The Go-Between*. London: Penguin, 1953.

Haught, John F. *The Revelation of God in History*. Wilmington, DE: Michael Clazier, 1988.

"History and Narrative." *Musalaha*. 20 February 2017. http://www.musalaha. org/articles/2017/2/20/history-and-narrative.

Jones, Adam. *Genocide: A Comprehensive Introduction*. New York: Routledge, 2006.

Kidner, Derek. *The Message of Ecclesiastes*. Leicester, UK: Intervarsity, 1976.

Lewis, C. S. *Mere Christianity*. New York: HarperOne, 1952.

Lewry, Osmund. *The Theology of History*. Notre Dame, IN: Fides, 1969.

Lindsay, Hal. *The Late Great Planet Earth*. Grand Rapids, MI, 1970.

Lockner, Louis P. *What about Germany?* New York: Dodd, Mead & Co., 1942.

Marshall, I. H. *The Epistles of John*. Grand Rapids, MI: Eerdmans, 1978.

McCullough, David. *John Adams*. New York: Simon & Schuster, 2001.

Moltmann, Jürgen. *History and the Triune God: Contributions to Trinitarian Theology*. New York: Crossroad, 1992.

Ortlund, Raymond C. *Isaiah: God Saves Sinners*. Wheaton, IL: Crossway, 2005.

Ricketts, Paul. "Move in Our Midst." *Friends Journal*. http://www.friendsjournal. org/move-in-our-midst.

Santayana, George. *The Life of Reason, or, The Phases of Human Progress*. New York: Scribner, 1905.

Scott, Joan Wallach. *Gender and the Politics of History*. New York: Columbia University Press, 1988.

Smuts, Adriaan. "Amnesty Application." *Truth and Reconciliation Commission*. 12 August 1996. Transcript. http://www.justice.gov.za/trc/ amntrans%5Cdurban/smuts.htm.

Snyder, Timothy. *Black Earth: The Holocaust as History and Warning*. New York: Tim Duggan, 2015.

Spurgeon, C. H. *The Treasury of David: An Original Exposition of the Book of Psalms*. Peabody, MA: Hendrickson.

Stump, Eleonore. *Wandering in Darkness: Narrative and the Problem of Suffering*. Oxford: Oxford University Press, 2010.

Tolkien, J. R. R. *The Lord of the Rings: The Fellowship of the Ring*. New York: DelRey, 2012.

Tutu, Desmond, and Mpho Tutu. *The Book of Forgiving: The Fourfold Path for Healing Ourselves and Our World*. San Francisco: Harper One, 2014.

Waalkes, Scott. *The Fullness of Time in a Flat World: Globalization and the Liturgical Year*. Eugene, OR: Cascade, 2010.

White, Hayden. *Metahistory: The Historical Imagination in Nineteenth Century Europe*. Baltimore: Johns Hopkins University Press, 1973.

Zinn, Howard. *A People's History of the United States*. New York: Harper and Row, 1980.